Out the back, down the path

COLORADO OUTHOUSES

Kenneth Jessen

with articles by
Charles Collins, Mary Jane Groves, Cheryl Miller, Thomas Noel, Ed Quillen and Merle Rust

J. V. Publications L.L.C.

OUT THE BACK, DOWN THE PATH: COLORADO OUTHOUSES

Copyright© 2002 by Kenneth Jessen

No part of this book may be reproduced, stored in a retrieval system or transmitted in any form, or by any means, electronic, mechanical, photocopying, recording or otherwise without prior written permission of the publisher.

Published by J. V. Publications, LLC, 2212 Flora Court, Loveland, CO 80537 USA
Printed in the United States of America

First Edition
1 2 3 4 5 6 7 8 9

Publisher's Cataloging-in-Publication *(provided by Quality Books, Inc.)*
Jessen, Kenneth Christian.
    Out the back, down the path : Colorado outhouses / by
Kenneth Jessen ; with articles by Charles Collins ...
[et al.]. -- 1st ed.
    p. cm.
    Includes bibliographical references and index.
    LCCN 2002190310
    ISBN 1-928656-03-X

    1. Outhouses--Colorado.   I. Title.

TD775.J47 2002   728'.9'09788
                        QBI02-200713

Cover painting by Richard Schilling (www.WorldWideWatercolorist.com). Book design and production by LaVonne Ewing. Editing by Susan Hoskinson. Interior illustrations by Kenneth Jessen except where noted. Photography by Tony Bluma, Charles Collins, Mary Jane Groves, Kenneth Jessen, Benjamin Jessen, Sonje Jessen, Keith Maull, Ardie Schoeninger, S. Dean Sneed and Cyndi Trombly.

To my wonderful family,
Andrew, April, Ashley, Ben, Chris,
Dusty, Mariah, Sonje and Todd

Acknowledgements

Thanks to LaVonne Ewing for her book design and to Susan Hoskinson for editing this work. In addition, I would like to thank my many contributors, including Charles Collins, Mary Jane Groves, Cheryl Miller, Tom Noel, Ed Quillen and Merle W. Rust for their articles; Richard Schilling for his cover watercolor painting; and Tony Bluma, Charles Collins, Mary Jane Groves, Sonje Jessen, Benjamin Jessen, Keith Maull, Ardie Schoeninger, S. Dean Sneed and Cyndi Trombly for their photographs. A special thanks to S. Dean Sneed for his help on the coal camp section and to Lyle Miller for information on the Salt Works Ranch privy. In addition, I would like to thank Phillip Flores and Allen White for help in developing the section on composting comfort stations.

About The Author

Kenneth Jessen is author of a dozen books, 700 articles and several booklets. He has a weekly column in the Loveland *Reporter-Herald* and is a contributor to *Lydia's Style Magazine, Colorado Central Magazine, North Forty News* and *Colorado Time-Table*. His articles also have appeared in *True West, Frontier Times, Old West, Trains, Rail Classics* and *Colorado Heritage*.

Jessen is a life member of the Colorado Railroad Museum, longtime member of the Rocky Mountain Railroad Club, centennial member of the Colorado Historical Society, member of the Summit Historical Society, patron of the San Luis Valley Historical Society, Westerners International and one of the founders of the Western Outlaw-Lawman History Association.

He has appeared on KCNC-Channel 4's *Colorado GetAways* with his ghost town stories and has been a guest on both commercial and public radio. At the present time, Jessen has a monthly radio show on KCOL 600 AM. On two different occasions, Colorado State University selected Jessen for its American West Program. He has appeared twice as part of the Colorado Historical Society's lecture series and twice as part of the Greeley Museum's evening lecture series at Centennial Village.

Educated with both a bachelor's degree and a master's degree, Jessen spent 36 years as an engineer for Hewlett-Packard and Agilent Technologies.

Sonje Jessen is a major contributor to his books and acts as editorial consultant. She also was instrumental in locating and photographing many of the ghost towns on various field trips. The couple lives in Loveland, Colorado, and they have three grown sons, two daughter-in-laws and three grandchildren.

Kenneth Jessen owns and operates J. V. Publications L.L.C., with the objective of publishing books of regional interest that encompass the Rocky Mountain West.

sketch by Richard Schilling

Table of Contents

Map 8
Introduction 9
Definitions 9
Slop Jars and Where Potatoes Are Grown 10
Crescent Moon 12

Chapter 1. Northern Colorado
Facilities and Utilities by Merle W. Rust 14
    Barnes Meadow Construction Camp 17
    Buckhorn Canyon Privies 18
    Columbine 19
    Cowdrey: Sheet Metal Privy 20
    Hahns Peak Privies 21
    Horsetooth Privy Prowler 23
    Jackson County Outhouse Tour 24
    Lohr/McIntosh Farm Privy Could Be Cleaned 25
    McGraw Ranch: Outhouse to Telephone Booth 26
    Pearl 27
    Rocky Mountain National Park: Cub Creek Privy 28
    Virginia Dale Stage Station Privy 29
    Virginia Dale Community Church Privy 30

Chapter 2. Eastern Colorado
City Could Solve All of Its Financial Woes by Mary Jane Groves ... 32
    Alvin: A Town of Many Locations 35
    Beecher Island 36
    Chivington, Named for a Villain 37
    Clarkville 38
    Dailey: Church Privy 39
    Eckley: Sheet Metal Chamber 40
    Fleming: Railroad Outhouse 41
    Grover: Custom-Built Privy 42
    Heartstrong 43
    Idalia 44
    Joes: Three Men Named Joe 45
    Keota 46
    New Haven 47
    Raymer 48
    Sheridan Lake 49
    Sidney 50
    Snyder: Combined Coal Shed and Privy 51
    St. Petersburg 52
    Vernon 53
    Wauneta: Community Center WPA Sanitary Privy 54
    Weldona 55
    Willard 56

Chapter 3. North-Central Colorado
Boulder County Privies
    Eldora: Nicest Looking Outhouse in Colorado 58
    Gold Hill: Privy in the Trees 60
    Nederland: Brick Privy 61
    Salina 62
    Sunshine Schoolhouse Outhouses 63
    Wall Street 64
    Ward 65
Clear Creek County Privies
    Dumont School: Matching Outhouse 66
    Empire: All WPA Sanitary Privies 67
    Georgetown: Home to Colorado's Most Ornate Outhouse 68
    Lawson 70
    Silver Plume: Flush in Outhouses 71

Gilpin County Privies
- Black Hawk: From Mills to Gaming ... 72
- Central City ... 74
- Mountain City: Site of First Gold Discovery ... 75
- Nevadaville: Bald Mountain Post Office ... 76
- Rollinsville ... 77
- Humorous Outhouses at Russell Gulch ... 78

Chapter 4. Central Colorado

Eagle County Privies
- Fulford: Probable Periscope Privy ... 80
- Gilman: On the Edge ... 81
- Red Cliff ... 82

Outhouses in the Clear Creek Drainage
- Rockdale: Less Than Sanitary Privy ... 83
- Vicksburg: Tree-Lined ... 84
- Winfield ... 85

South Park Outhouses
- Alma ... 86
- Alma Junction Privy ... 87
- Como: Boys' and Girls' Privy ... 88
- Fairplay: Leaning Outhouse ... 89
- Guffey: Bill Soux, Outhouse Builder ... 90
- Hartsel: Unique Schoolhouse Privy ... 93
- Salt Works Privy ... 94
- Tarryall Schoolhouse Privies by Cheryl Miller ... 96

Summit County Outhouses
- Boston: Attached Outhouse ... 98
- Breckenridge: Alice Milne Privy ... 99
- Dillon: Site Now Under Water ... 100
- Frisco: Historic Park Privy ... 101
- Lincoln City: Steel Outhouse ... 102
- Montezuma's Revenge ... 103
- Pennsylvania Mill and Peru Creek ... 104
- Slate Creek Hall Ventilated Privies ... 105
- Wapiti: Extra Tall Outhouse ... 106

Teller County Outhouses
- American Eagles Mine ... 107
- Anaconda: Fallen Outhouse ... 108
- Goldfield: Varied Outhouses ... 109
- Theresa Mine Privy Required Courage ... 111
- Victor: Decorative Tin Privy ... 112

Upper Arkansas Valley Outhouses
- Camp Cree: Massive Log Privy ... 113
- Crystal Lakes Schoolhouse Privy ... 114
- Derry Ranch and Its Violent Past ... 115
- Finntown: Once Had a Six-sided, Corrugated Steel Privy ... 117
- Futurity ... 118
- Granite: Modified WPA Sanitary Privies ... 119
- Inter-Laken: Hexagonal Outhouse ... 120
- Leadville: Outhouse Race ... 122
- Malta School Outhouse ... 123
- Mary Murphy Mine: Depositors Had to Walk the Plank ... 124
- Oro City: Home of H. A. W. Tabor ... 125
- St. Elmo: Colorado's Popular Ghost Town ... 126
- Turret: No Uninvited Depositors ... 127
- Twin Lakes: Formerly Called Dayton ... 128

Chapter 5. South-Central Colorado

Coal Camp Privies
- Cokedale: Coal Sheds ... 130
- Engleville: WPA Sanitary Privy on Rails ... 132
- Hastings ... 133
- Ludlow Massacre Site ... 134
- Redstone ... 135
- Rockvale ... 136
- Tollerburg: Privies That Could Be Cleaned ... 137
- Valdez ... 139

Vallorso 140
Custer County Outhouses
  Old-time Outhouse Is Going Way of All Flush by Ed Quillen ... 141
  Beckwith Ranch Outhouse 145
  Bishop's Outhouse 146
  Westcliffe 148
Gunnison County Outhouses
  Alpine Tunnel 149
  Crested Butte: Two-Story Outhouses 150
  Crystal: Known for Its Power Plant 153
  Iris 154
  Marble 155
  Pitkin: Depot Privy 156
  Sandy Hook 157
  Tincup: Many Privies 158
San Luis Valley Privies
  Bonanza: Extra Tall Outhouse 159
  Fort Garland: Railroad Outhouse 160
  Garcia 161
  Jaroso: Kircher's Outhouse Offers Best Television Reception . 162
  Lobatos 163
  Los Rinecones Morada 164
  Mesita: Mormon Church Privy 165
  San Francisco 166
  Summitville 167
  Viejo San Acacio 168

Chapter 6. Western Colorado
  Alta 170
  Bedrock 171
  Capitol City: Lee Mansion Privy 172
  Cortez 173
  Dove Creek 174
  Dunton 175
  Gateway 176
  Lake City 177
  Red Mountain Pass 179
  Silverton: Moyle Brothers Band 180

Chapter 7. Composting Comfort Stations
  Grizzly Creek 182
  Colorado's World-Class Outhouse by Thomas Noel 184
  Maroon Creek 186

Appendix A
Great Plains Privies by Charles Collins 189

Appendix B
Review of Selected Outhouse Books 199

Bibliography 201
Index 204

Map of Selected Colorado Towns

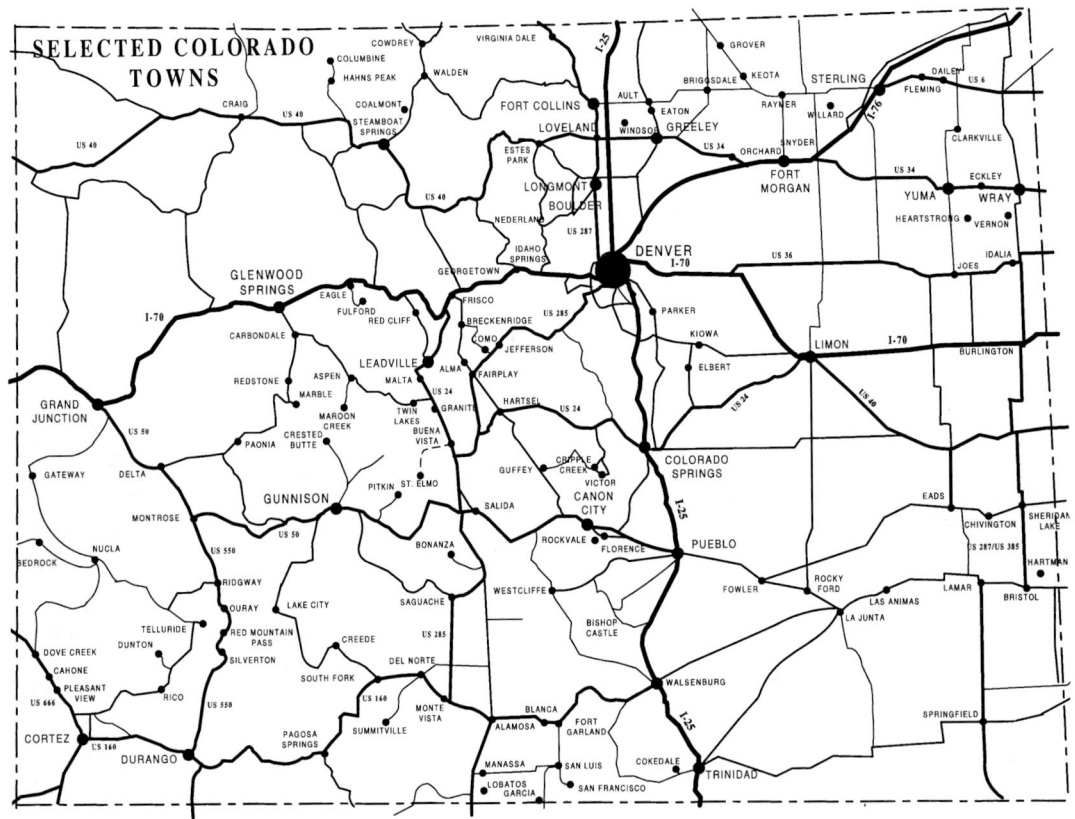

Definitions

Webster's New Collegiate Dictionary provides definitions for several words used interchangeably for outhouse. They are not sugarcoated.

OUTHOUSE: outbuilding; esp. privy
PRIVY: a small building having a bench with holes through which the user may defecate or urinate.
LOO: Toilet (esp. British)
DUNNY: Outdoor toilet (esp. Australian)

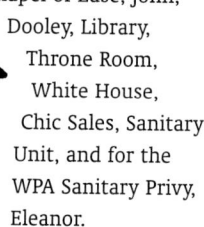

Other words for an outhouse: Nessy, Biffy, Chapel of Ease, John, Dooley, Library, Throne Room, White House, Chic Sales, Sanitary Unit, and for the WPA Sanitary Privy, Eleanor.

Introduction

Hundreds of outhouses are spread out over Colorado. This book focuses on a selection of unique structures, ordinary structures in extraordinary settings and structures rich in history. It also incorporates the ideas of others to properly place the privy as part of American culture, by illustrating its evolution from a wooden structure over an unlined pit, to a concrete-lined pit and finally to an ecologically sensitive modern composting comfort station.

The privy at Old Maid Mine near Dexter Creek north of Ouray is an example of an ordinary structure in an extraordinary location. (Ardie Schoeninger)

SLOP JARS AND WHERE POTATOES ARE GROWN

My interest in outhouses was not voluntary. As a boy, I spent the summers at my grandparents' Virginia home where there was no indoor plumbing. Modesty took precedent over practicality, and the outhouse was located behind both a trellis fence and barn. Not only was the structure hidden from the road, it could not be seen from any place in the house. A plank walkway curved around the barn and led to the outhouse. The planks were laid on the ground and were slippery when wet. Slugs, making their way across the planks, added to the hazard. At a distance of well over 100 feet, visitors needing relief had to ask for directions.

For the brave, a kerosene lantern was available for nighttime trips. Unescorted trips by children were out of the question after sunset. To solve an obvious problem, each bedroom was equipped with a chamber pot, more commonly called a slop jar. Every morning, it was someone's distasteful task to go into the bedrooms and retrieve the slop jars. They were then carried to the outhouse, emptied and washed at the outdoor spigot.

One morning, an unlucky family member lost her grasp on one of the slop jar handles at the top of the stairs. Each tread had an L-shaped piece of metal on its edge, and as the slop jar tumbled

Displayed at the Red Cliff Museum, this slop jar is similar to those used within many households. Each bedroom was equipped with a slop jar or chamber pot for nighttime relief. (Kenneth Jessen)

end-over-end, it made a tremendous noise. Its contents were disgorged as the porcelain-clad metal container accelerated toward the bottom, followed by the lid. Since the children were often relegated to clean-up duty, all fled from the house to the surrounding farmland to return later in the morning.

The outhouse was a simple, wooden structure built by my grandfather and designed to be moved periodically. There was a Sears and Roebuck catalog inside, as well as toilet paper. A bucket of lime with a scoop sat in the corner to be used to reduce flies and odor. It was a two-holer: one hole for children and the other for adults, neither very comfortable. There were rectangular screen vents on both sides and a hook-and-eye latch on the inside. The entire structure was painted white inside and out.

Since the door opened outward, a common prank was to run by and tug on the handle. If the occupant had failed to use the inside latch, the door would swing open beyond reach. The helpless occupant would be left exposed.

For dinner, garden-fresh potatoes were part of the daily meal. All of the food was homegrown, and the milk came directly from a cow kept in the pasture. Refrigeration was achieved by keeping the food in crocks submerged in cold, spring water that circulated through the spring house.

During one meal, the adults discussed how excellent the potatoes tasted. The conversation turned to where the potatoes were grown. It was revealed that the previously abandoned outhouse pit was the site of the potato patch. Up to this time, the children had not known that the outhouse was relocated periodically. The next morning, the children investigated, and the potato patch was in fact located in a small depression about 50 feet above the outhouse. The following evening, as was customary, garden-fresh potatoes were served. Remembering where the potatoes were grown, the children refused to eat them for the remainder of the summer.

Mollie Harris, in *Privies Galore*, wrote about Mavis Brown. When Brown was a child, she used to stay in the country with her aunt and uncle. She noticed that the inside of the earth-pit privy was decorated with prizes for the best vegetables for miles around. There were also prizes for roses, chrysanthemums and many other flowers. She would sit there entranced, reading them and noting that there were first prizes for almost everything. Brown finally asked her aunt why she pinned them up in the privy, and her aunt replied, "Well, what comes out of the privy goes on the garden to grow the fruit, vegetables and flowers that wins us the certificates, so I reckon that's where they should be, where the credit lies."[1]

As was common in farming communities, my grandparents' outhouse was placed along a path that led by the coal shed so that users could take care of business, then bring back a scuttle full of coal. If an individual had to be excused, he might say he needed to get some coal, meaning he was headed to the outhouse and did not wish to be joined by other family members.

The children invented a railroad game, and each location in the yard was given the name of one of the surrounding towns. Abingdon, for example, was in the front yard, and Emery was along the side of the house. The Norfolk & Western Railroad had a branch to a town called Saltville, and that was the designation for the outhouse since it was on a dead-end path. When any of the children wished to be excused, they would say they were going to Saltville. Visitors would look puzzled, but family members would understand.

1. Mollie Harris, *Privies Galore*, (United Kingdom: Alan Sutton, date unknown), p. 22.

CRESCENT MOON

A crescent moon carved into an outhouse is the commonly accepted symbol for the structure. One outhouse myth is that during the 1500s, two different symbols were used to differentiate a men's facility from a women's facility. The crescent has long been used for women, while the sun represents men. The story goes that men failed to provide proper privy maintenance and also were more casual about their bodily functions than women. Over time, only the women's privy survived, and by default, the crescent moon became the symbol for an outhouse.

Dottie Booth in her book, *Nature Calls*, tells that porcupines caused the demise of men's outhouses. They would enter and gnaw away at the seats causing the structure to eventually be abandoned. The urine on the seats is what attracted the incisor-equipped little animals. To add credence to this story, the seat in the Squaw Peak outhouse has been gnawed away.

This is all nonsense since in the 1500s, few could afford separate facilities. Historians state that the crescent moon always has been the symbol for an outhouse.

chapter 1

OUTHOUSES OF

NORTHERN COLORADO

To provide relief prior to horseback riding, this outhouse is at the stables in Glen Haven, located near the North Fork of the Big Thompson River. (Kenneth Jessen)

FACILITIES AND UTILITIES
by Merle W. Rust

As a little boy growing up in Northern Colorado, I thought everyone in the world used an outside toilet. How was I to know otherwise? Being seventh of eight children, that little building was the center of the universe for quite a few of my early years. It had to be moved one time—the supply was too far ahead of demand. Paper had something to do with that, I suppose, because pages from a Montgomery Ward catalog do not deteriorate as quickly as "modern" toilet paper. That soft paper wrapped around the hollow stick was for rich, city folks.

For little boys, a privy does not present many problems. Of course my sisters had a whole different set of circumstances, but my brothers and I could always find a tree, barn corner, or post that always needed a little extra water. The final trip to the "little house" before bedtime was always a traffic jam and pretty exciting at times. The girls usually came back to the house on the run, out of breath, and either screaming or giggling. Usually they had just seen a man lurking in the shadows or some hideous monster that missed, only by an inch, of capturing one of

An early toilet paper ad from a Montgomery Ward catalog notes that 100 rolls of "No. 1 quality" could be purchased for $7.50. (Mary Jane Groves collection)

them. Brother John and I would have little brother, Don, frightened to the point that he virtually had to be pushed out the door carrying his flashlight. He would then search every nook, cranny and tree with a beam of light before relieving himself in record time and making it back to the house at just under the speed of light. Of course, extreme winter weather necessitated a convenient gallon can at the foot of each bed.

During World War II, Dad took it upon himself to bring the family into the real world with a bathroom and running water in the house. The fact that the war effort made building supplies virtually unobtainable, the project seemed to take forever. An old porch was torn down and a kitchen-family room replaced it. The room that had served as a kitchen became our new, modern bathroom. A long ditch was dug toward the river and a leach field constructed for drainage. A total of four 55-gallon drums were filled with river rock to act as leachfields. Part of my contribution to the

Generally, an outhouse does not have any surprises. This unit is near the Great Stupa of Dharmakaya, a Buddhist temple near Red Feather Lakes. The surprise is that the toilet seat is propped against an interior wall, and the floor is a solid sheet of plywood. (Kenneth Jessen)

project was to carry rocks from the riverbed to fill these drums. A new wood and coal range was moved into the newly constructed room. It not only had a reservoir for hot water, but also a "water jacket" in the firebox to circulate and store hot water in a holding tank. It worked like a charm—as long as a fire was burning. The best was still to come! A new sink was installed in the kitchen, and all the bathroom fixtures were hooked up to hot and cold running water. This would replace the old hand pump in the old kitchen. A pressure tank was in our fruit and vegetable cellar hooked to the fixtures and our storage cistern. It was ingenious, and it worked.

Were these "good of days" really as good as we portray them? No, I think not, but it certainly doesn't hurt anything to be a little reminiscent of our past and savor telling "stories" to today's little ones. Where will we go if we don't know where we've been!

From *Big Tales from the Big Thompson Valley* by Merle W. Rust. Self-published, 1996. Reproduced by permission of the author.

Even businesses have involved the privy. The Old Privy was located in Heritage Square in Golden. As shown in this 1976 advertisement, it sold bathroom accessories. (Arlene Ahlbrandt collection)

BARNES MEADOW CONSTRUCTION CAMP

Old log buildings and an outhouse remain standing along Colorado 14 west of Fort Collins near Barnes Meadow Reservoir. These structures were erected around 1922 as a construction camp for workers who were building the reservoir. Financed by Roy Portner, the reservoir inundated the old David Barnes homestead. David Barnes was prominent in Colorado history for founding the town of Loveland in 1877.

Barnes Meadow Reservoir construction camp outhouse. (Sonje Jessen)

BUCKHORN CANYON PRIVIES

The Dukart outhouse may be the most decorated privy in Colorado. It is located on private property above the Buckhorn Canyon and includes such features as a sink, external light, birdhouse, hanging flower pot, part of a cast iron stove and bed-frame railing. Since the Dukart's do not have neighbors within sight of their outhouse, there is a large window on the right side to provide natural lighting. This outhouse is equipped with reading material, such as Harry Walker's definitive work, *Outhouses of Alaska*.

Possibly Colorado's neatest outhouse, complete with vacuum cleaner, is the Ewing outhouse. A small lean-to in the rear hides the propane tank for the Ewing cabin. The interior includes carpeting, and the outside is nicely finished in wood paneling.

Dukart's Buckhorn Canyon outhouse. (Kenneth Jessen)

Note the vacuum cleaner just inside the door of the Ewing's Buckhorn Canyon outhouse. (Kenneth Jessen)

COLUMBINE

To support nearby mines around Hahns Peak, Columbine acted as a supply center beginning with construction of a general store in 1880. The town was officially laid out in 1897, but already had gained its own post office the year before. Mining lasted until the early part of the twentieth century, at which time the dozen or so cabins were abandoned.

With the construction of a dam to expand Steamboat Lake, tourism began to dominate the area economy. The town of Columbine was purchased and converted into a resort. The original cabins were repaired and rented to summer visitors, and new guest cabins were added. Columbine continues to operate as a resort today.

It present owners have preserved much of the town's original character. Several outhouses have been restored, but are no longer in use. Other privies remain "active."

Columbine privy and aspen tree. (Kenneth Jessen)

COWDREY: SHEET METAL PRIVY

Charles Cowdrey homesteaded in North Park in 1882 after having viewed the area on a hunting trip the year before. He moved from his ranch to establish the town of Cowdrey in 1901, the same year the town got a post office. Cowdrey ran a store and meat market. The small town also had a hotel and livery stable. It was difficult to make a living. This prompted Cowdrey to move to Carson City, Nevada, in 1904. His town, however, continues to survive today along Colorado 125. A sheet metal "his" and "hers" outhouse sits behind a modern steel building, although the outhouse is much older. It possibly served a commercial building in Cowdrey. Old car bodies surround the structure.

Sheet metal privy in Cowdrey. (Kenneth Jessen)

HAHNS PEAK PRIVIES

When Hahns Peak residents Gail and Gary Garneau discovered that two historic outhouses in nearby Columbine were going to be burned, they moved the structures to a vacant lot next to their home. The Garneaus went to work decorating the privies and did such a nice job that their privies are a tourist attraction.

Longtime Hahns Peak residents Rilla and Al Wiggins replaced their original outhouse behind their historic cabin with "Big John." Bright red, it sits by a weathered shed. The Wiggins operate the small store along Hahns Peak's main street.

The schoolhouse at Hahns Peak was constructed in 1911. It operated until the end of the 1940-1941 term. By this time, all children in the area lived west of town. The county superintendent had a portable schoolhouse constructed, and a team of horses pulled it to several different sites. The Hahns Peak schoolhouse and its two privies were abandoned. The structures were listed on the National Register of Historic Places in 1974 and form the core of historic structures in the town.

Garneau privy, located in Hahns Peak. (Kenneth Jessen)

The town and the peak are named for German immigrant Joseph Hahn. He and several partners discovered gold in the area. An expedition of fifty men was organized to explore the area. As the winter of 1866 approached, Hahn stayed behind with William Doyle and Capt. George Way. Way was sent for supplies with a pouch filled with gold dust. He never returned, and to avoid starvation, Hahn and Doyle set out on snowshoes for civilization. Hahn perished, and Doyle was rescued by a couple of cowboys.

"Big John" located behind Wiggins cabin in Hahns Peak. (Kenneth Jessen)

Hahns Peak was the only population center in Routt County for many years and became the county seat in 1901. Hahns Peak remained the county seat until 1912 when voters elected to move the offices to Steamboat Springs.

HORSETOOTH PRIVY PROWLER

Privy at Horsetooth Mountain Park near Fort Collins. (Kenneth Jessen)

Outhouses are generally safe from prowlers. The word privy, commonly used interchangeably for outhouse, means "private; not public." In June 1988, a woman using the facility at Horsetooth Mountain Park, west of Fort Collins, noticed the telltale red light of a video camera below in the depths of the vault. When she looked down, she saw Robert Thomas Cobabe standing in sewage. He was wearing hip waders and plastic bags. She screamed, and he fled through a manhole.

Brave investigators took fingerprints at the crime scene in an effort to get a match with known privy prowlers. But the investigation stalled. While the police were looking, Cobabe earned a bachelor's degree in human development and family studies at Colorado State University. After he graduated, Cobabe enrolled at Regis University to take coursework required for earning a teaching certificate. As required by Colorado state law, he was fingerprinted. After his prints were processed, there was a match with the set from the Horsetooth Mountain Park crime scene. This led to Cobabe's arrest January 5, 2000. He was charged with second-degree burglary and third-degree sexual assault. Without mandatory fingerprint matching, Cobabe could have become a teacher in a school system.

JACKSON COUNTY OUTHOUSE TOUR

What does a library do to purchase books when there is no state, county or municipal funding? Volunteers for the Friends of the Jackson County Library came up with the idea of having a tour of North Park barns and outhouses in 1996. Each stop on the tour includes a narration about the historical significance of the property. After the tour, a barbecue is held at the Wattenberg Center, north of Walden. Attendees are treated to good food and live music, courtesy of an all-female, seven-piece jug band. Songs about outhouses and chamber pots are included in the selections. One of the musical instruments consists of a gilded toilet seat with tuned washers suspended by strings to create a wind chime sound.

The 2002 tour included a stop in Walden where property owners Kris and Rex Shaw displayed their pair of oversize outhouses rescued from a business located in town. The interiors were elaborately decorated with stuffed moose, stove and even a bed in one of the structures. The Shaw family, dressed in formal attire, considered it only appropriate for such an event. Other properties on the tour included century-old barns in North Park at the Lozier, Wattenberg and Lone Pine ranches.

Rex and Kris Shaw, dressed for the 2002 Friends of the Jackson County Library barns and outhouse tour. (Kenneth Jessen)

Interior of a Shaw outhouse in Walden. (Kenneth Jessen)

LOHR/MCINTOSH FARM PRIVY COULD BE CLEANED

Lohr/McIntosh farm privy west of Longmont. (Kenneth Jessen)

Farmers are a practical sort. They try to keep life simple, and this philosophy applies to their outhouses. A small, lightweight wooden structure will do fine for most farmers. Many times they construct their privy from scrap material. When the pit is full, the structure is slid or carried to a new pit.

At the Lohr/McIntosh farm, however, this didn't apply. This privy is a rare example of one with a hinged door in the back to provide access to a removable wooden waste trough. To reduce the smell associated with a non-pit style outhouse, lids were placed over each of its two holes. The Lohr/McIntosh farm is operated as an agricultural heritage center by Boulder County, and its outhouse is being restored. Judging from the capacity of the waste trough, it probably had to be cleaned often. The explanation for this type of privy lies in the rocky soil where pit digging is simply not practical.

The Lohr/McIntosh farm is located between Longmont and Lyons on the south side of Colorado 66. It not only includes this unique privy, but the picturesque 1881 McIntosh barn, 1909 Lohr farmhouse, circa 1900 Dickens barn, silo, milk house, windmill, granary and other structures. The buildings are the product of George McIntosh, who settled on the land in 1868, and George Lohr, who purchased the farm in 1899.

McGRAW RANCH:
OUTHOUSE TO TELEPHONE BOOTH

John and Irene McGraw came to Estes Park in 1907 on their honeymoon. After visiting the Double Bar Y ranch, they signed a 25-year lease. After two years of living on the property, the McGraws exercised their option to purchase the ranch.

Tourism began to dominate Estes Park during the late nineteenth century. Access roads were improved, and in 1915, Rocky Mountain National Park was opened. The McGraws raised cattle, but in 1935-1936, they decided to provide guest accommodations, and cabins were constructed.

An outhouse was constructed on the hillside above the ranch house, centrally located among the guest cabins. After indoor plumbing was installed in the guest cabins, the outhouse was converted into a telephone booth. A solid bench replaced the one with toilet seats. On the exterior, a "stick style" rustic trim of narrow tree branches has been added.

In 1988, the National Park Service purchased the McGraw Ranch. The structures have been either restored or renovated, depending on their historical status.

McGraw Ranch telephone booth converted from outhouse near Estes Park. (Kenneth Jessen)

PEARL

Pearl, located in extreme northwest North Park, is one of Colorado's least known mining camps. Its economy was based on copper mining, and a smelter was constructed at the south edge of town.

The Wheeler brothers were first to settle in the area. Although copper ore was discovered in 1894 - 1895, it took five years to develop the mines. The post office opened in 1889 with Pearl Wheeler the first postmaster. The town was named for her. In 1901, the town took its first steps toward incorporation with an election. The following year, the town had its own government and included twenty-three structures covering fourteen city blocks.

Only a few original structures remain today, and most of the cabins are seasonally occupied. Most of the cabins have outhouses. The town itself is on private property and is off limits to visitors. The smelter collapsed years ago, but its smokestack remains standing.

Note the double hip roof on the outhouse in this group of ranch buildings on the Pearl town site. (Kenneth Jessen)

ROCKY MOUNTAIN NATIONAL PARK: CUB CREEK PRIVY

What may be a case of false privy advertising is located along the Cub Lake Trail in Rocky Mountain National Park. On the main trail there is a wooden sign engraved with "privy," an arrow and the neat outline of an outhouse with a roof, door and half moon. The actual structure fails to even approach what appears on the sign.

The case of false privy advertising. (Keith Maull)

Deep in the woods, but within sight of the campground are two slab-wood walls about four-feet tall set at right angles. Where the walls form a corner is the toilet. It is supported on a piece of plywood over the pit. This privy is anything but private. It is exposed to weather, visitors and wild animals. The lack of a structure around the toilet reduces the smell, but not summertime insects. Since it is exposed to the elements, toilet paper cannot be left behind. It is, therefore, a "BYOTP" style of privy.

This privy fails to provide any sense of sanitation or security. It is not a place to sit and think, or even linger. In all fairness to the National Park Service, there are many such privies in the national parks, some a lot less private. It is better than no privy at all!

Cub Creek open air privy in Rocky Mountain National Park. (Keith Maull)

VIRGINIA DALE STAGE STATION PRIVY

Did Jack Slade use this privy? Although it is located behind the historic Virginia Dale Stage Station, constructed by the Central Overland California & Pikes Peak Express Company in 1862, this outhouse is too new.

Jack Slade had a bad reputation for killing men and even removing their ears. He was in charge of a vast portion of the Overland route that provided transcontinental stagecoach service through the Rocky Mountains. Slade established Virginia Dale as the division headquarters when the line was moved from its original route through central Wyoming to the south to take advantage of the growing traffic in the Denver area. Located near Dale Creek, he named the place for his wife, Maria Virginia. The privies can be seen in the distance behind the 1862 Virginia Dale stagecoach station.

The station is listed on the National Register of Historic Places and is one of Larimer County's most important historic sites.

Virginia Dale Stage Station and outhouses. (Kenneth Jessen)

VIRGINIA DALE COMMUNITY CHURCH PRIVY

Virginia Dale Community Presbyterian Church and its functional outhouse. (Kenneth Jessen)

The small Virginia Dale Community Presbyterian Church has a solitary outhouse in the back, and it is still functional. The church was constructed in 1879 on nearby Table Mountain Ranch, and then in 1884, it was moved to its present location. The church is a log structure with its exterior covered with clapboard siding, and the outhouse is a frame structure.

chapter 2

OUTHOUSES OF

EASTERN COLORADO

"CITY COULD SOLVE ALL OF ITS FINANCIAL WOES"
by Mary Jane Groves

No one is suggesting we return to yesterday's plumbing. Still, nostalgia about the old days is a persistent theme in American culture. The passion for privies, in part, stems from a shift in preservationist priorities to include structures from everyday life. After all, the "little white house" played a key role in mankind's well being.

An inside look at American innovation and hang-ups reveals that residential privies were most often of the two-hole variety. Many had provisions for young children in the form of built-in steps, smaller holes and pots for nighttime use. Enlightened builders included hinged seat covers, but unattached lids of all varieties were also popular.

The seats in the outhouse at the Kitzmiller Ranch in the sandhills of northern Yuma County are decorated with the names of those who use the facility. Note the corncobs, an uncomfortable alternative to toilet paper. (Mary Jane Groves)

These edifices were subject to vigorous weekly cleaning routines, being scrubbed with the leftover soapy wash water and brooms. Decor consisted of wall calendars as well as prints or pictures from favorite magazines, box tops and other common materials used to insulate the walls. Some even had decorated seats.

The heyday for the little houses arrived when official concern about rural health and sanitation resulted in the construction of what were called WPA sanitary privies. Between 1933 and 1945, over two million sanitary privies were available to homeowners for the cost of materials (about $35 for one-holers) through the Federal Works Progress Administration. Building such a large number of these structures put many men back to work during the Great Depression.

A concrete pit or vault with a riser equipped with a pine seat and lid was recommended. Many farmers simply dug holes in the ground for their sanitary privy. To them, portability was important in privy construction. When the pit was full, the farmer could simply dig a new hole and drag the little house over it.

In 1940, even though housewives threatened a mass march on Washington and an Anti-Snooping club was formed, the federal census takers wanted to be privy to such personal details as the number of outhouses. They ascertained that more than fourteen million homes were still using the little house behind. Most of these were in rural communities and were in use by two of every three households. In contrast, 83 percent of urban homes had indoor toilets. As late as 1989, there were at least four million privies doing business in backyards from Maine to California.

The end to outhouses for most towns came with the construction of a sewer system. In Wray, located in the eastern part of Yuma County,

This simple, little white house is located at the Lucas Cemetery west of Idalia, Colorado. (Mary Jane Groves)

This classic WPA sanitary privy sits behind the community building at Wauneta. (Mary Jane Groves)

a construction bid was accepted in 1920 for Sewer District No. 1. After July 1, 1941, it became unlawful to maintain any building or place where people reside that is not provided by a flush toilet connected to the sewer system or a sanitary, fly-tight privy approved by the Colorado State Board of Health. In 1961, the City of Wray declared all privies, closets, or other outhouses of similar nature a nuisance and menace to public health. The city ordered them demolished, punishable by a fine not exceeding $300, with each succeeding day constituting a separate offense.

As of the year 2001, the city could solve all of its financial woes by enforcing this ordinance on the three buildings that still exist. This would be 40 years times 365 days times $300 per day times the three structures amounting to a little over $13 million.

The "seat of democracy" is fast vanishing from America's backyards. In the post-Victorian era, many well-meaning preservationists often demolished the objectionable backhouse on historic sites. Thus, scores of perceptive school children ask the same question, "Where did all the people who lived here go to the bathroom?"

These days, however, the old outhouse is in. Those that were once routinely burned or torn down are now sold to the highest bidder, moved and restored. Now we're more aware of their history and architecture and the importance of preserving structures from everyday life.

Originally presented as part of a slide show under the title "Diamonds in the Rough" and reproduced with the author's permission.

ALVIN: A TOWN OF MANY LOCATIONS

Alvin was founded in 1910 by A. A. Currence with the intention of running a combination store and post office. Currence purchased the land from Alvin Davis, and as a condition of the sale, Davis stipulated that the place be named Alvin. The store at Alvin prospered. When the business was sold, the store and post office were moved to the Jim Coast homestead, a short distance away. Coast eventually sold the store, and Alvin moved again. Another sale took place, and Alvin moved once again. Possibly worn out by all the moves, a new store was constructed in 1918. In 1929, the post office was closed. Eventually, Jim Miles purchased the Alvin store and moved the building 3 miles east at the intersection of 51 RD and RR RD where Alvin's abandoned buildings rest today. The site is only 1.5 miles west of the Nebraska line.

A fallen outhouse sits among the ruins of the small settlement of Alvin, located in the sandhill region of Yuma County. (Kenneth Jessen)

BEECHER ISLAND

Not only is this the site of a historic battle between soldiers and Native Americans, it was also a small town with a chapel, auditorium, museum and store. Originally called Glory, its post office opened in 1924. The following year the name was changed to Beecher Island.

The site is dominated by the large auditorium. The auditorium seems out of place in this remote location. It was constructed in 1927, and the nearby chapel was built in 1950. There are a number of outhouses at the site, some to serve visitors to the memorial and others to serve the auditorium.

Outhouse at Rim Rock southwest of Beecher Island. Note the remnants of a shake shingle roof. (Mary Jane Groves)

Outhouse near auditorium at Beecher Island. (Mary Jane Groves)

CHIVINGTON: NAMED FOR A VILLAIN

Chivington was named for Col. John Chivington, one of the true villains in Colorado history. It seems appropriate that this town is all but abandoned. Chivington, a Methodist minister, marched his Colorado volunteer cavalry to Sand Creek in 1864 where peaceful Cheyenne and Arapahoe men, women and children were camped. These people had been promised protection by the U.S. Army and flew an American flag. Chivington's men opened fire despite cries for mercy. After the slaughter, the bodies were mutilated. Later, Chivington received a hero's welcome in Denver.

The town of Chivington was established southwest of the Sand Creek massacre site along the Missouri Pacific. The railroad constructed a roundhouse, and the town was incorporated in 1888. Today, Chivington's business buildings are abandoned, and the schoolhouse is on the verge of collapse. Only a few people call this place home.

Outhouse west of abandoned business district in Chivington. (Kenneth Jessen)

CLARKVILLE

Clarkville community center has two WPA sanitary privies, both have been pushed over. Original wooden roofs were replaced by corrugated steel. (Kenneth Jessen)

At one time, Clarkville had a store, gas station and post office. These structures are gone. Remaining structures include the schoolhouse, now used for storage, and the community center with its tipped over outhouses. A modern church and one home also occupy the site. Clarkville's population stands at three.

Clarkville began in 1933 with the home of Harry Nielsen and his Texaco filling station. The filling station included a small store. In 1936, the filling station was sold to Ted Clark. When the post office opened two years later, the location became Clarkville. Fred Rigby, an early pioneer, once commented about the number of residents named Clark, "If you meet anyone on the road, you need not ask his name for it would be Clark and he would have come from Smith County, Kansas."

Ted Clark added to the structures by moving a building from Haxtun, and later the church was moved to Clarkville. With the consolidation of area economic centers, the population of Clarkville fell, and the post office closed in 1954. The filling station went out of business and was sold at auction in 1961.

DAILEY: CHURCH PRIVY

How this small town got its name is uncertain, but it was founded at the time a railroad siding was established in the early 1900s. A general store opened in 1915 followed by a school and grain elevator. The Dailey State Bank opened its doors in the early 1920s. The church at Dailey was abandoned after its congregation merged with the Methodist Church in Haxtun. The grain elevator closed in 1985 and had been the town's source of employment. Today, Dailey is partially abandoned.

Three-hole outhouse sits behind an abandoned church in Dailey. (Kenneth Jessen)

ECKLEY: SHEET METAL CHAMBER

In its push westward, the Burlington & Colorado Railroad, a subsidiary of the Chicago, Burlington & Quincy, reached the Eckley site by the end of

Abandoned building in the once bustling business district of Eckley. (Kenneth Jessen)

1881. The following year, the railroad continued construction through Fort Morgan to Denver. Although a temporary town may have been formed at the end of the tracks, Eckley was not surveyed until 1889 by the Lincoln Land Company. It was named for Adams Eckles, foreman of a local ranch.

This sheet metal outhouse in Eckley looks like a bomb shelter. Lack of ventilation indicates that the interior gets quite hot during the summer, and users probably leave the door open. (Kenneth Jessen)

FLEMING: RAILROAD OUTHOUSE

The Nebraska & Colorado Railroad (a subsidiary of the Chicago, Burlington & Quincy, now the Burlington Northern-Santa Fe) entered Colorado in 1887. They selected a place 29 miles west of the Colorado/Nebraska border and called it 29 Mile Siding. A small community formed at the siding and was renamed Calvert for a railroad superintendent. The following year, Henry Bascom Fleming arrived in the area and settled a mile west of Calvert. Fleming donated the land for a town site, and the town of Fleming was established. Businesses in Calvert moved to Fleming, and Fleming grew until the dust bowl of the 1890s. The United States suffered a depression in 1893 and many moved away, but by the start of the twentieth century, prosperity returned to Fleming.

In the 1980s, the depot, which had been retired by the railroad, was moved to a historic park along with its outhouse. The outhouse was placed on the ground, not over a pit, and forms part of the museum display.

Outhouse behind the Fleming depot. (Kenneth Jessen)

The Chicago, Burlington & Quincy depot at Fleming. (Kenneth Jessen)

GROVER: CUSTOM-BUILT PRIVY

This attractive, well-maintained custom-built privy in Grover is one of several still standing in the town. (Tony Bluma)

Grover was founded along the Burlington & Missouri as a water stop at approximately the same time as the towns of Willard and Keota. It was originally called Point of Rocks, and when the postmaster had to pick a name for the post office, his daughter selected her mother's maiden name, Grover. The post office opened in 1885, but the town was not platted until three years later. The settlement grew to include several stores, two hotels, stockyards, three lumberyards, two livery stables and a blacksmith shop. It also had a newspaper, the *Tri-City Press*. The railroad was abandoned, and the rails were removed during the 1970s. The two-story depot now serves as an area museum.

HEARTSTRONG

This now-abandoned community has one of the strangest histories in the state. Cleve Mason and his brother-in-law, Clarence Gilmore, started a store in Happyville. Mason sold the store to a co-operative and built an even larger store. The two-story structure included a garage, grocery store and post office on the ground floor. The second floor was used as Happyville's dance hall.

Things were not always happy in Happyville, however. Mason was angered over a dispute with other residents. In 1921, he resigned as postmaster and founded a new town 2 miles to the west. He called it Heartstrong. Using ninety-six horses, he moved his two-story building to Heartstrong. He also moved three houses to the new town leaving Happyville with hardly a structure. Soon, the Happyville post office closed, the town was abandoned and mail was delivered to Heartstrong. The drought during the early 1930s started Heartstrong on a downhill slide. Its post office closed in 1940, and only foundations remain at the site today.

Tipped over outhouse near Heartstrong site. (Kenneth Jessen)

IDALIA

Two outhouses merged into one at Idalia. (Mary Jane Groves)

Idalia is a thriving Yuma County agricultural community blessed with good farmland. The community was originally called Alva, but the name was changed in 1888 to Idalia. Stories vary as to how the town was named. One account says it was named for three pioneer women; another claims it was named for Ida Lee Helmick. Ida Lee was simplified to Idalia. The original town consisted of a hotel, hardware store, post office, livery stable, lumberyard and saloon. The Idalia State Bank was established, and the *Idalia Republican* supplied residents with the local news for a number of years. With changes in the area roads, Idalia was moved about .5 mile southwest in 1911-1912.

One outhouse at Idalia made of two separate structures served a café at the Colorado Department of Revenue check and weigh station near Idalia.

JOES: THREE MEN NAMED JOE

Some sources say that the town of Joes was named for three men, each named Joe. In 1910, when an application was made for a post office, the name listed was "Three Joes." Postal officials rejected the name in favor of just Joes. The post office opened in 1912.

In 1929, the town had but forty residents, yet its basketball team placed first in state. The team went on to place third in nationals and put their small town on the map.

A corrugated steel outhouse at the community park in Joes has been replaced by a modern cinderblock structure. The old privy has separate mens' and womens' sections, each with its own door.

Corrugated steel outhouse at Joes. (Kenneth Jessen)

KEOTA

The abandoned town of Keota is another reminder of attempts to settle Eastern Colorado with ranching and dryland farming. Like Willard, Keota was founded in 1888 along the Burlington & Missouri, a subsidiary of the Chicago, Burlington & Quincy. A railroad station was constructed, and the town had an imposing hotel as well as a two-story schoolhouse. By 1918, Keota was a thriving community along the railroad and reached a peak population of 140. As area roads improved, towns like Keota started to decline. The Great Depression and the Dust Bowl sent Keota on its final downward spiral. The bank failed in 1923, the hotel closed, and by 1936, Keota had a population of 108. The high school closed in 1951, and by 1970, only seven residents were left, including the editor of *The Keota News*, Clyde Stanley. When James Michener wrote his epic, *Centennial*, Stanley provided valuable insight into the area. For this, Stanley's name appears in Michener's dedication.

North of Clyde Stanley's building are a couple of outhouses. The business district in Keota is completely abandoned, and only one family lives near the town site. Now the water tower stands as a sentinel over the once thriving community.

Abandoned outhouse near Keota water tower. (Tony Bluma)

NEW HAVEN

In 1910, the Bellvue school was constructed at this site. The small town that grew up around the school got its post office in 1911 under the name New Haven. The name came from the fact it was a haven for those in poor health. The town once had a church and even a community orchestra. With the exception of a grain elevator, the businesses at New Haven are gone. The school closed in 1962. Grandparents of the first female astronaut, Sally Ride, lived in New Haven and were town pioneers.

WPA sanitary privy among farm buildings at New Haven town site. (Kenneth Jessen)

RAYMER

One of two abandoned outhouses behind a commercial building in Raymer. Raymer is north east of Greeley on Colorado 14. (Tony Bluma)

It is rare in the history of Colorado towns that one is completely abandoned and its buildings razed to be later reoccupied on exactly the same site. Emma Courtright, a dressmaker, purchased land for the proposed town of Raymer in 1888 for $187.09. It was located along the tracks of the Burlington & Missouri Railroad. The town grew to have a business district, homes and a railroad depot. Hard times, however, caused the businesses to close during the 1890s, and in 1895, the Raymer post office closed. The buildings were razed, and the lumber was used by area ranchers.

A new settlement was platted in 1908 on the same site. The post office was re-established in 1909 under the name "New Raymer," and today, this small town is kept alive by agriculture and traffic along Colorado 14. The "New" has been dropped, and maps now show the town as simply Raymer.

SHERIDAN LAKE

Originally, Sheridan Lake was the town of Bee, an alphabetical naming system proposed by Jessie Mallory Thayer, the daughter of the president of the Pueblo & State Line Railroad. Bee was passed over by the railroad for a station, so the residents constructed their own. Bee's depot was successful, and the agent at the nearby town of Arden was eventually transferred to Bee.

Soon after the railroad's arrival in 1887, the name Bee was dropped, and the town of Sheridan Lake was incorporated as a real-estate development scheme. The nearby buffalo wallow was promoted as a beautiful lake, and the place was said to have been Gen. Phil Sheridan's favorite camping spot. The only truth is that Sheridan did march through the area.

Sheridan Lake became the Kiowa County seat until Eads won the title by popular vote. Before the matter was officially settled, the people in Eads stole the county records by using a locomotive and a flat car. Even the building used for county offices was moved to Eads. Today, several outhouse stand at Sheridan Lake. Partially abandoned, most of the town's business buildings are in ruins.

Privy near a vegetable garden in Sheridan Lake. (Kenneth Jessen)

SIDNEY

WPA sanitary privy near schoolhouse site in Sidney. (Kenneth Jessen)

The area 6 miles south of Elbert in Kiowa County was settled by Philip P. Gomer in 1869. He was in the timber business and opened a lumber camp and sawmill. The place was called Gomer's Mill, and in 1870, it got its own post office.

In 1882, the economy of the area changed when the Denver & New Orleans constructed a standard-gauge line south from Denver through Parker and Elbert, ending in Pueblo. Gomer's Mill was called Bijou Siding by the railroad, but the name was soon changed to Sidney. The Denver & New Orleans was destroyed by a flood along Kiowa Creek in 1935. This ended economic growth in the area.

In 1962, John Dunn purchased the Sidney schoolhouse on 82 RD that had served not only as a school but also as the United Brethren Church. After its use as a school from 1888 to 1935, it became a residence. Its original outhouse was replaced during the 1930s by a WPA sanitary privy. Adjacent to the property are two homestead cabins built in the 1860s.

SNYDER: COMBINED COAL SHED AND PRIVY

One man in Snyder, Mr. Williams, is proud of his outhouse. Although he uses it as a storage shed, he keeps it painted and in good repair. The door on the left is to the toilet section, and the door on the right is to the coal shed. To add to its authenticity, his son hung an old catalog in the outhouse with several pages torn off as a reminder of "country" toilet paper.

Snyder got its start in 1881 with the arrival of the Union Pacific Railroad. The town was the center of operations for the Iliff Cattle Company, and when its owner, John Iliff, passed away, J. W. Snyder was appointed administrator of the estate. The town was named for Snyder. The post office opened in 1882, and the town was platted in 1897. During its peak, Snyder had a business district consisting of two general stores, newspaper office, drug store and depot.

After the railroad was abandoned, the Union Pacific depot was razed along with three section houses for railroad workers. The beet scale house still stands, but little else remains of the town's agricultural industry.

Neatly painted outhouse in Snyder. (Kenneth Jessen)

ST. PETERSBURG

The dominant structure in St. Petersburg is St. Peter Catholic Church. Just south of the town site is the cemetery. The town still has several residents, but the school sits abandoned. The community center next to the church is well maintained, including its pair of WPA sanitary privies.

WPA sanitary privy in St. Petersburg, complete with a windbreak. (Kenneth Jessen)

St. Petersburg abandoned schoolhouse. (Kenneth Jessen)

VERNON

Vernon, located southwest of Wray, is one of the neatest, best looking towns in Eastern Colorado. When the town was platted in 1892, its five founders couldn't decide on a name. To settle the issue, they asked the local Methodist minister, Rev. James J. Vernon, to pray on the issue. As if they got a message from above, they decided to use the reverend's surname, Vernon.

At the time the town was platted, Boatman and York already had opened a store. Soon Vernon had a hotel and livery stable. A schoolhouse was built plus several churches. Vernon also gained a post office. In viewing the town's original plat, Vernon is about the same size as it always has been. Vernon only has a couple of outhouses, thanks to a sewage system.

Farm outhouse on south edge of Vernon. (Kenneth Jessen)

Vernon business district. (Kenneth Jessen)

WAUNETA: COMMUNITY CENTER WPA SANITARY PRIVY

WPA sanitary privy behind the community center in Wauneta. (Kenneth Jessen)

Behind the community center at Wauneta is an outhouse among playground equipment. The town is located in the sandhill region 15 miles north of Wray in Yuma County along U.S. 385.

The town started around the home of Sidney Atwood, who operated a blacksmith shop. Store owner Pat Dempsey was dating Atwood's daughter Wauneta. Dempsey named the community Wauneta, and later the couple was married.

WELDONA

Weldona has its share of abandoned businesses and homes, like so many small towns in Eastern Colorado. The railroad depot has been restored, however, and there are some fine, older homes in the town. Weldona is located northwest of Fort Morgan along Colorado 144.

Abandoned store fronts in Weldona. (Kenneth Jessen)

Abandoned Weldona outhouse in a grove of trees. (Kenneth Jessen)

WILLARD

Located east of Greeley on the prairie is the partially abandoned town of Willard. Daniel A. Willard was an official of the Chicago, Burlington & Quincy and quit to become the president of the Baltimore & Ohio. The town was named for this man, and it was incorporated in 1888 along the Burlington & Missouri, a subsidiary of the Chicago, Burlington & Quincy. Willard flourished for many years and had a small business district, school and church. The consolidation of farms and ranches and the diminished need for rail service spelled the end to Willard's prosperity. By 1960, there was only intermittent service on the railroad, and the line was completely abandoned during the 1970s. Although the Methodist Church remains active, only a few people live in the town. The Mahorey combination store and post office was closed in 1967.

Top: One of the few outhouses in Willard.

Right: Mahorey combination store and post office in Willard. (Kenneth Jessen)

chapter 3

OUTHOUSES OF

NORTH-CENTRAL COLORADO

Bill Pierson's outhouse located on the east end of Eldora on private property. (Kenneth Jessen)

Boulder County Privies

ELDORA: NICEST LOOKING OUTHOUSE IN COLORADO

Eldora got its start in 1889 when John A. "Jack" Gilfillan ventured over the mountains from Caribou in search of gold. On Spencer Mountain near today's Lake Eldora Ski Area, Gilfillan built a cabin and staked out the Clara claim. Possibly due to the heavy snowfall, Gilfillan decided to move to the base of Spencer Mountain. Here, he constructed a second cabin at the future site of the town of Eldora. When placer mining attracted hundreds of prospectors, Gilfillan decided the place had become too crowded and began numbering each log in his cabin. He moved the structure, log by log, to the side of Eldorado Mountain where he could watch the hustle and bustle from a distance.

In 1897, the town got its own post office under its original name "Eldorado." The town's population was about 300 at the time, and tents were giving way to permanent structures. By the beginning of the following year, the new town reached a population of 1,300.

As the volume of mail increased, the postmaster noticed many letters were undeliverable. Upon close examination, these letters were addressed to "Eldorado, CA." and not to "Eldorado, CO." To eliminate the confusion, the Postal Service requested that the town change its name. The "do" was dropped, and the town became Eldora.

At the east end of Eldora and behind his century-old log home, Bill Pierson constructed what may be the nicest looking outhouse in all of Colorado. The outhouse is of pleasing proportions with a small front porch and short stairway from ground level. He built the outhouse in the early 1980s to replace an older unit that included a coal shed. Bill designed the outhouse as he went and now believes that he got carried away. The home has been in the Pierson family since 1909.

Eldora's "Glory Hole" on a side road on the south side of Middle Boulder Creek. (Kenneth Jessen)

Boulder County Privies
GOLD HILL: PRIVY IN THE TREES

Gold Hill outhouse in grove of trees. (Kenneth Jessen)

Gold Hill is the first permanent mining town in the Colorado mountains. Practically all other mountain towns are located either in a canyon or on a hillside. Gold Hill is on the top of a divide and can be reached by any of four roads.

The first gold discovery in the area was made in 1859. Gold Hill was the economic center of the district, and at the time, it was located within Nebraska Territory.

The gold was easy to recover and came in the form of flakes in decomposed quartz. Gold Hill's population soon swelled to 1,500. As this surface ore was exhausted, many miners began to leave, and the town was partially abandoned. The town swelled with people again when miners began drilling into the rock and found more gold ore. Gold Hill faltered once again after the gold ore was exhausted. By 1870, only one mine remained in operation, and only six people called Gold Hill home.

Today, Gold Hill is one of the best-preserved mining towns in Colorado. It gives visitors a genuine feeling of how a Colorado mining town once looked.

Boulder County Privies
NEDERLAND: BRICK PRIVY

Nederland's two-hole brick outhouse. (Kenneth Jessen)

Nederland is located east of Eldora at the junction of Colorado 119 and the Peak-to-Peak Highway (Colorado 72). The first town built on this site was Dayton, but since it was located on Middle Boulder Creek, the post office was named Middle Boulder. A large mill was constructed at the west end of town to process the ore coming from Caribou. The mill was purchased by a Dutch mining company, and they renamed the town Nederland. The post office followed suit in 1874.

Brick and stone outhouses are rare. Once the pit is filled with offending material, a frame outhouse can be picked up and moved or skidded to a new location. Not so with more permanent structures. Periodically, the pit must be mucked out, a highly distasteful job.

Behind a brick home that was once a doctor's office is a matching brick outhouse. It can be assumed that the good doctor wanted something more permanent than the typical wood-frame outhouse common in the rest of Nederland. The house is now a coffee shop.

Boulder County Privies

SALINA

Restored Salina schoolhouse and its two outhouses. (Kenneth Jessen)

The Salina schoolhouse was constructed in 1875. There are two well-kept outhouses to the side, and the school is open for community affairs.

The town was founded by seven men from Salina, Kansas, and by 1873, thirty families called Salina home. The placer deposits were soon exhausted, but hardrock mining began with the discovery of rich gold ore. By the time the school was constructed, the town had more than 100 residents. Salina had stores, saloons, assay office and three mills. The Salina House was the town's hotel. The Colorado & Northwestern constructed a narrow-gauge railroad from Boulder through Salina in 1898 and gave the town a boost. Lower-grade ore and concentrates could be shipped economically to Boulder for processing.

Mining and milling was discontinued long ago, but Salina was never completely abandoned. It now serves a number of residents, and its remaining historic structures have been preserved.

Boulder County Privies
SUNSHINE SCHOOLHOUSE OUTHOUSES

The beautiful stone Sunshine School was constructed in 1900 to replace a wood-frame schoolhouse. The building was entered on the National Register of Historic Places in 1981 and restored in 1991. Fortunately, the historic "his" and "hers" outhouses on the hillside behind the schoolhouse were left in place.

The stone Sunshine School, constructed in 1900. (Kenneth Jessen)

Interior of one Sunshine School outhouse. (Keith Maull)

Boulder County Privies
WALL STREET

The problem one Wall Street owner had with his outhouse was that it was located on the opposite side of the road from his home. A person in a hurry could be struck by a passing car on the way to the privy.

A short distance west is the imposing foundation of the Gold Extraction Mining and Supply mill, constructed in 1902 to process gold ore from local mines. The town of Wall Street was laid out in 1898 near the mill and consisted of six city blocks, but only a handful of people ever called it home. The mill closed two years later, and the mine was sold at a sheriff's auction.

Modest structure across road from Wall Street home. (Kenneth Jessen)

Privy behind the Wall Street assay house. (Kenneth Jessen)

Boulder County Privies
WARD

A devastating fire in 1900 destroyed fifty-three of Ward's buildings, including most of its business district. The structures were never rebuilt, and only a small percentage of their value was covered by insurance. The town did not die, however, and it remains occupied today. The schoolhouse serves as the town's post office and library. Its boys' and girls' outhouses remain functional. The white clapboard community church also survived the fire and dominates the town site. A quaint outhouse sits on the hillside opposite the church.

The town was originally named Columbia City, but the name was changed to Ward for Calvin M. Ward, who discovered the Miser's Dream. Incorporated in 1896, Ward got rail service two years later with the arrival of the narrow-gauge Colorado & Northwestern. Rail transportation allowed low-grade ore to be recovered economically. Mining continued well into the twentieth century. Ward's peak population was about 600.

Abandoned outhouse opposite Ward's community church. (Kenneth Jessen)

Clear Creek County Privies
DUMONT SCHOOL: MATCHING OUTHOUSE

Brick privy within full view of I-70 conforms to architectural style of schoolhouse. (Kenneth Jessen)

Interior of decommissioned schoolhouse privy at Dumont. (Kenneth Jessen)

The outhouse behind the Dumont schoolhouse in Clear Creek County is kept clean and functional. However, sanitation officials warned Mill Creek Historical Society volunteer Chuck Harmon that such outhouses were banned. In order for the schoolhouse to continue to serve as a place for social functions, inside plumbing was added, and the outhouse was officially decommissioned.

The outhouse is made of light-colored brick to match the Dumont schoolhouse and has a windbreak on the west side where the doors are located. It has separate boys' and girls' toilets, each with two holes. The schoolhouse and its matching outhouse were constructed in 1909. Both the privy and schoolhouse are listed on the National Register of Historic Places.

Clear Creek County Privies
EMPIRE: ALL WPA SANITARY PRIVIES

The town of Empire is located west of Denver along U.S. 40 and on the east side of Berthoud Pass. An exit off of I-70 provides easy access to the town.

Empire was settled in 1860 when George Merrill and Joseph Musser constructed a cabin at the confluence of Bard Creek, Lion Creek and the West Fork of Clear Creek. Originally named Valley City, the town company dissolved, and the camp remained unnamed for several weeks. The name "Empire City" was suggested by a settler from New York, the Empire State. In 1886, "City" was dropped, and the town became Empire.

During the 1930s, someone must have done a great job selling the folks in Empire on the WPA sanitary privy. There are at least a half-dozen still standing, and no custom-made outhouses remain.

Discarded WPA sanitary privies in Empire's alleys. (Kenneth Jessen)

Mike Lopez owns an excellent example of a WPA sanitary privy. Painted pink, he uses it for storage. The structure is in perfect condition with a concrete slab, concrete riser supporting the toilet seat and box vents.

Clear Creek County Privies
GEORGETOWN: HOME TO COLORADO'S MOST ORNATE OUTHOUSE

No book on outhouses would be complete without the elaborate six-hole Victorian privy behind the Hamill House in Georgetown. It has a divider between the servant's side and the family side, which acts as a plenum up to its elaborate cupola. The servants got to use pine toilet seats, and the family enjoyed walnut seats. The seats on both sides, however, are smooth and well finished.

When William Hamill's brother-in-law, Joseph Watson, left Georgetown, Hamill moved his family into Watson's simple, two-story home. From 1874 to 1881, Hamill used the wealth he gained in silver mining to transform the home into the largest, most elegant mansion in Georgetown. He hired architect Robert Roeschlaub, known for the design of other Victorian homes in Georgetown, to add to the Watson home. One of the most impressive rooms built at

Elaborate cupola on Hamill House outhouse functions as a vent. (Keith Maull)

The Hamill House Victorian privy measures 148.5" wide and 121" tall to fascia board.

the time was a solarium. In 1879, a chateau-style office building and a carriage house were constructed on the property. The outhouse probably dates to that year. The structure is located in Georgetown, west of Denver near I-70, and the Hamill House is operated as a museum open to the public.

Servant's side of Hamill House outhouse. Openings were different calibers to accommodate adults and children. (Kenneth Jessen)

Hamill House outhouse in Georgetown. (Kenneth Jessen)

Clear Creek County Privies
LAWSON

Discarded WPA sanitary privies sit in the weeds at the east side of Lawson.
(Kenneth Jessen)

Lawson was founded by an ambitious young man named Alex Lawson. He operated a stagecoach line between Denver and the towns along Clear Creek. In the town of Lawson, he built the Six-Mile House. It served meals to stagecoach passengers. The town grew to 500 and had four stores, school, post office and several churches. Still standing is the saloon constructed by Adolph Coors. It was later purchased by Walter E. Anderson and converted into a combination grocery store and gasoline station.

Clear Creek County Privies

SILVER PLUME: FLUSH IN OUTHOUSES

Silver Plume is flush in outhouses, both active and abandoned. The town was founded in 1870 based on the numerous silver mines immediately above the town site. Much of Silver Plume was destroyed by fire in 1884, but it was quickly rebuilt. A subsidiary of the Union Pacific, the Georgetown, Breckenridge & Leadville, reached Silver Plume in 1884 over a spectacular railroad called the Georgetown Loop. Later, the Argentine Central was constructed from Silver Plume to serve the mines at Waldorf. It was extended to over 13,000 feet above sea level as a tourist attraction.

I-70 splits Silver Plume into an upper portion and a lower portion. The north end of Silver Plume is confined by a near-perpendicular cliff. The cliff provides a spectacular backdrop for outhouses in this part of town.

It is a cold trip to this Silver Plume outhouse. (Kenneth Jessen)

Silver Plume outhouse next to cliff. (Kenneth Jessen)

Gilpin County Privies
BLACK HAWK: FROM MILLS TO GAMING

Black Hawk and the surrounding towns all owe their existence to John H. Gregory's gold discovery on May 6, 1859, on the western boundary of Black Hawk. In fact, the State of Colorado was originally founded on such discoveries.

Whereas Central City evolved into a town of businesses, hotels, saloons and homes, Black Hawk, with a good supply of water from the North Fork of Clear Creek, became the mill town. The town was served by two railroads, and its better-off residents lived in Chase Gulch. Constant noise of stamp mill and smelters rang out 24 hours a day, and sulfur-laden smoke obscured visibility.

The town got its name from a mill constructed in 1860, and a couple of years later, the town got its own post office. Black Hawk was incorporated in 1864, and soon reached a population of 2,000.

The hike up to the Black Hawk schoolhouse requires ascending eighty-seven steps from Gregory Street. The school now serves as police headquarters. Its outhouse has separate sections for boys and girls. It probably dates to the construction of the schoolhouse in 1870.

Black Hawk schoolhouse outhouse, constructed in 1870. (Kenneth Jessen)

Abandoned outhouse on hillside above Gregory Street in Black Hawk. (Kenneth Jessen)

After the end of the mining era, Black Hawk was almost abandoned, and many of its buildings collapsed or were razed. It was regarded as a poor sister to Central City. After legalized gambling began on October 1, 1991, all of this changed. Black Hawk moved from mill town to ghost town to Colorado's largest gaming town. In the process, every available square inch along Main Street was converted into casinos or parking lots. What few structures remained were moved to a historic park on Gregory Street.

The Lace House is one exception. It sits on an isolated pedestal of original hillside held together by walls fabricated with concrete sprayed over wire mesh. The Lace House is considered Colorado's finest example of Carpenter Gothic architecture with its elaborate gingerbread trim. The house and its outhouse were built in 1863 for Lucien K. Smith, tollgate keeper for the road to Empire. The structures are listed on the National Register of Historic Places. The outhouse is located at the end of a wooden staircase making a midnight winter trip an uncomfortable, hazardous and memorable experience. It can be safely assumed that the Smith's owned an ample supply of chamber pots.

Top: Lace House outhouse in Black Hawk. The gray material in foreground is concrete sprayed over wire mesh to hold hillside.

Left: Lace House surrounded by parking lots and roads for Black Hawk's casinos. (Kenneth Jessen)

WPA sanitary privy on private property in Central City. (Kenneth Jessen)

Gilpin County Privies
CENTRAL CITY

Between 1933 and 1945, the WPA funded the construction of over two million "sanitary privies." Most of them were installed in the South, but a few made their way West. This is the most common type of outhouse left in Colorado. Its characteristics are the wide fascia board, single sloping shed roof and door offset to one side. A concrete slab and riser support the toilet inside most WPA sanitary privies. The toilet sits at a 45-degree angle with a wooden box vent behind the seat.

A view of Central City taken in 1864 shows the back of its business district with outhouses behind almost every building. Each outhouse sits on stilts, so that all waste products dropped into Gregory Gulch. After Central City's business district was destroyed by fire in 1874, new structures made of brick and stone replaced frame construction. Sanitation also improved.

Although started in 1859, Central City did not come into its own until 1861 when the Territory of Colorado formed and the town became the Gilpin County seat.

Gilpin County Privies

MOUNTAIN CITY: SITE OF FIRST GOLD DISCOVERY

Mountain City was the site of the first lode discovery containing gold ore in Colorado. It was made on May 6, 1859, by John H. Gregory. This and other discoveries led to the permanent settlement of Colorado by non-Native Americans. Mountain City was formed around the Gregory Mine and was the site of the first religious services in Gilpin County. The town had a Masonic Temple, log theater and about 200 cabins of various sizes. For a brief time, it even had a weekly newspaper. Mountain City eventually was absorbed into Central City.

There were several brick buildings located along Gregory Street, including the Kruse Grocery Store. Behind the home adjacent to the store was the family outhouse on a steep hillside. A steep staircase provided access. Visits during the night, especially after a heavy snowfall, must have proved challenging.

Central City photographer H.H. Lake photographed Mountain City between 1865 and 1875. Note staircase that leads to outhouse behind the home right center. (Denver Public Library)

Gilpin County Privies
NEVADAVILLE: BALD MOUNTAIN POST OFFICE

Nevadaville was founded three weeks after John Gregory's gold discovery in 1859, and the town was initially known as Nevada or Nevada City. After a post office was established, it became apparent that there was confusion with a town by the same name in California. Some mail destined for "Nevada, CA" ended up at "Nevada, CO" or vice versa. In 1869, the post office opted to change the name to Bald Mountain, but residents called their home Nevadaville.

By 1860, Nevadaville had 2,705 residents making it slightly larger than Denver. The end of its boom years came with the discovery of rich, silver ore in 1879 near Leadville, and Nevadaville began to lose population. Several of the town's original structures survive.

A modern outhouse serves residents of a stone house located near Nevadaville. (Kenneth Jessen)

Two outhouses, photographed in the 1930s, next to abandoned mining structures in Nevadaville. Note two boards prop outhouse in the background. (Denver Public Library)

Gilpin County Privies
ROLLINSVILLE

Located along Colorado 119, Rollinsville is where the highway crosses over Union Pacific tracks. The Rollinsville stage station now serves as a restaurant, and an old, abandoned store sits nearby.

John Q. A. Rollins invested in Gilpin County gold mines and commercial salt works in South Park, and he constructed a toll road over Rollins Pass to Middle Park. He also owned 2,000 acres of farmland and extensive placer deposits. Rollins founded Rollinsville, and on a bench above town, he constructed a mill in 1861 to process gold ore from his mines. A decade later, the town got a post office. Other businesses were established in Rollinsville, but isolation hampered their development.

Outhouse and abandoned buildings in Rollinsville. (Kenneth Jessen)

On the west side of Colorado 119 is a row of abandoned buildings. On the left is an outhouse. The buildings are near the foundation of an icehouse that was once used to supply railroad cars with fresh ice prior to the days of mechanical refrigeration.

Gilpin County Privies
HUMOROUS OUTHOUSES AT RUSSELL GULCH

Russell Gulch, located on the graded dirt road between Central City and Idaho Springs, is one of the earliest mining camps in Colorado. The town was founded around the 1859 cabin of William Green Russell, one of Colorado's pioneer prospectors. It was once home to 2,000 individuals, and at the time, it had a main street lined with stores. Today, Russell Gulch is a ghost of its former self with only a few residents living among its abandoned buildings.

Behind the schoolhouse is a unique outhouse built on top of a stone wall and covered with sheet metal siding. The foundation wall forms the pit. Its builders were forced to use an above-ground pit due to the rocky nature of the hillside.

Lacking a sewage system, the outhouse is still part of daily life in Russell Gulch. Its residents show a unique sense of humor by decorating their outhouses with signs and other objects, such as a TV antenna.

A sandwich sign over the entrance is combined with a radiation hazard sign and a TV antenna on Russell Gulch outhouse. (Kenneth Jessen)

A "Stop, Dead End" sign on outhouse in Russell Gulch. (Kenneth Jessen)

chapter 4

OUTHOUSES OF

CENTRAL COLORADO

Eagle County Privies

FULFORD: PROBABLE PERISCOPE PRIVY

This remote mining camp, located above Brush Creek south of Eagle, was originally referred to as Nolan's Camp. The name came from an early prospector, William Nolan, who discovered rich ore in 1887. He didn't live to enjoy the fruits of his prospecting, however. While carrying a loaded gun, the trigger caught on a twig or limb and discharged. The gun was pointed straight up, and the bullet went through Nolan's tongue. He was alone and far from help. Nolan bled to death.

Based on rich ore discovered in 1890 by Dick Morgan, a town was laid in the meadow where Nolan's Camp was located. Morgan was joined by a local rancher, Arthur Fulford, and the place became known as Fulford.

Today, Fulford is a combination of a few original cabins and new mountain homes. Most have privies.

Sketch of privy designed by architect.

One outhouse in Fulford was designed by an architect. Its door faces the woods with a periscope aimed toward the house and Fulford's main street. Such a scheme works fine as long as the interior is relatively dark. One Fulford resident remarked that he could see its occupant at high noon.

Eagle County Privies
GILMAN: ON THE EDGE

Gilman is perched at the edge of a cliff 1,200 feet above the Eagle River. A nighttime trip to one of its outhouses could prove fatal. The camp began as Rock Creek, became Battle Mountain and then was named Clinton. It was formally laid out by Henry M. Gilman in 1886, and its name was changed to Gilman.

After the town's purchase by New Jersey Zinc in 1915, it took on a permanent character with nice clapboard-sided homes, stores, bowling alley and spacious schoolhouse. Millions of dollars in metals were recovered annually with the total topping $12 million in 1951. In 1981 with ore reserves depleted, the mine closed, and a Cañon City businessman purchased the entire town. In 1985, the sixty residents in Gilman were asked to leave due to water supply contamination. Since that time, the empty town is off limits on private property, but it can be seen from U.S. 24.

Gilman from U.S. 24. Note the outhouse on the left. (Kenneth Jessen)

One of few outhouses left in Red Cliff. (Kenneth Jessen)

Eagle County Privies
RED CLIFF

Below the spectacular high bridge that carries U.S. 24 over the Eagle River is the old mining town of Red Cliff. It dates to 1879 when miners from Leadville discovered silver ore in the area. The name, Red Cliff, was settled on by the prospectors and miners after the numerous red bluffs that dominate the site.

The Denver & Rio Grande constructed a narrow-gauge line from Leadville through the town in 1881. This was the terminus for the railroad until 1887 when the rails were extended westward. By this time, Red Cliff had three businesses, five hotels and a brass band to play at dances. It also had an opera house.

A sewage system and indoor plumbing spelled the end to Red Cliff's outhouses, and only a few representative examples are left today. With high demand for housing in the area driven by the recreation industry, almost all of Red Cliff's homes are occupied. In addition to a community center and city offices, Red Cliff also has a museum. With civic pride, it maintains its interesting, peaceful cemetery on the hillside above the town.

Outhouses in the Clear Creek Drainage
ROCKDALE: LESS THAN SANITARY PRIVY

East of Winfield on FR 390 is Rockdale, now property of the U.S. Forest Service. It superceded an earlier town, nearby Silverdale. Rockdale developed during the early 1880s supported by silver mining. As the price of silver dropped during the late nineteenth century, Rockdale was abandoned. The town shows signs, however, of recent occupation and possibly was used seasonally. There is an old slab-wood privy with its interior looking less than sanitary. A newer plywood outhouse sits nearby.

U.S. Forest Service now owns Rockdale, including these two outhouses. The privy on right is made of slab wood, and the other outhouse is of plywood construction. (Kenneth Jessen)

Outhouses in the Clear Creek Drainage
VICKSBURG: TREE-LINED

Vicksburg outhouse. (Kenneth Jessen)

In Clear Creek Canyon is one of the most beautiful mining camps in Colorado. Founded around 1880, its main street is lined on both sides with mature Balm of Gilead trees. The name of this town is Vicksburg, named for early prospector Vick Keller. Also unique are parallel community ditches on either side of the main street.

The town of Vicksburg has a parking lot just off of FR 390. A path leads to the town's small museum of mining equipment. Also included on the museum property is a ramshackle outhouse for visitors. Homes in Vicksburg are privately owned and seasonally occupied. Each house has its own outhouse.

Lattice screens privy entrance from prying eyes at Vicksburg. (Kenneth Jessen)

Outhouses in the Clear Creek Drainage
WINFIELD

The first cabin was erected in Winfield in 1861, but a town did not develop until later. As the mines were developed, Winfield's population reached well over 1,000. The town had a post office and school. The schoolhouse remains standing. It is open as a museum during the summer months and is operated by the Clear Creek Canyon Historical Society. Behind the school is its outhouse. Other cabins in Winfield are occupied during the summer, and their outhouses are, therefore, seasonally used.

Winfield schoolhouse with outhouse in back. (Kenneth Jessen)

South Park Outhouses
ALMA

Abandoned dual, "his" and "hers" outhouse once sat behind a commercial building on Alma's main street. (Kenneth Jessen)

What prompted the settlement of this area was the discovery in 1871 of silver ore at 13,860 feet on Mount Bross. Mining camps were set up, including Quartzville, Montgomery, Dudley and Buckskin Joe. One camp stood out, however, since it was at the lower elevation of 10,400 feet, where the winter weather was not quite as severe.

At this settlement, a local storekeeper suggested that the place be named for his daughter, Alma Janes. Alma was established in 1873 at the confluence of the Middle Fork of the South Platte River and Buckskin Creek. It survived while other camps were ultimately abandoned. The narrow-gauge Denver, South Park & Pacific constructed a branch to Alma in 1882 to service its smelters. After its population hit 900 in 1884, Alma began a steady decline as the price of silver dropped and area mines closed. Although most of its buildings were abandoned, a few people continued to live in Alma.

Today, new homes are being constructed in Alma, and many of its older cabins have been restored. Alma still has many outhouses, although most are no longer in use.

South Park Outhouses
ALMA JUNCTION PRIVY

Between Fairplay and Alma is Alma Junction (also called London Junction), a small town that formed where a branch of the Denver, South Park & Pacific narrow-gauge line left the main line for the London Mine. A depot was constructed in 1886, and 200 lived in the town. Many were railroad workers. Today, there are several restored cabins.

Outhouse and cabin at Alma Junction, located in South Park north of Fairplay. (Kenneth Jessen)

South Park Outhouses
COMO: BOYS' AND GIRLS' PRIVY

Snow-capped Park Range is setting for the Como boys' and girls' outhouse. Windbreak on right provided some protection from winter winds. (Kenneth Jessen)

Behind the schoolhouse in Como is a joined boys' and girls' outhouse. The town's history is tied to the construction of the Denver, South Park & Pacific. The railroad reached Como in 1879, and the town became a division point. The line over Boreas Pass to Breckenridge split off from the line to Leadville at Como. The Italian coal miners named the place after Italy's Lake Como.

Photographer Keith Maull captured the outhouse at the Denver, South Park & Pacific roundhouse in Como. (Kenneth Jessen)

South Park Outhouses
FAIRPLAY: LEANING OUTHOUSE

By August 1859, all of the gravel beds at Tarryall Diggings in South Park were staked out, and latecomers were turned away. Prospectors were unwilling to divide their generous claims, although only a few feet of river gravel could be worked at a time. The latecomers moved on and found a good placer deposit nearby. They named their town Fair Play, remembering the poor treatment they received at Tarryall Diggings. Fair Play, later simplified to Fairplay, became the largest town in South Park, and it is now the Park County seat.

After Fairplay got a sewage system, the old outhouses began to disappear. Now, outhouses are hard to find. There is one, however, on the south side of town behind an abandoned commercial building. It is leaning and will eventually fall over. It could be the last example of an outhouse in town.

Fairplay's leaning outhouse. (Kenneth Jessen)

South Park Outhouses
GUFFEY: BILL SOUX, OUTHOUSE BUILDER

Soux's "Roosters" and "Hens" outhouse behind the Guffey's city hall. Note the carpet in the front. (Kenneth Jessen)

Bill and Colleen Soux own much of the east end of Guffey, population thirty-five. They run the Guffey Garage and Last Chance Antiques. Soux also constructs unique outbuildings. Tired of traditional politicians, the town elected a golden retriever as its mayor. Voters wanted a change, and in the next election by a landslide, Monster became the new mayor. This is the Soux's black cat, and this gentle, good-natured animal makes a "purrfect" politician.

Soux constructed a "his" and "hers" outhouse beside the Guffey Garage and another twin outhouse behind city hall. He also restored his two WPA sanitary privies. All of the outhouses are kept spotless and odor-free.

Soux installed narrow, vertical interior mirrors in each side of his outhouses. On the men's side, the mirror is behind the toilet and on the women's side, it is mounted on a sidewall. They are positioned for maximum self-reflective impact. A second feature is the toilet seat hinge brackets made from polished horseshoes. Toilet paper holders are also of similar design.

The twin outhouse behind the city hall was built recently, and the seats are supported by part of a 55-gallon steel drum. To reduce the smell when the unit is not in use, Soux made lids that fit under the seat. Since earthen pits are no longer allowed in Park County, there is a 1,200-gallon holding tank below the structure. The partition between the men's and women's sides is made of planks. On the men's side only, there appears to be a large crack between the boards to allow peeping into the women's side. Through the crack can be seen the toilet and floor. Upon closer examination, however, it is not an error in outhouse construction, but a mirror. A potential voyeur sees only his face.

Soux added seat hinge brackets made from horseshoes to decorate his outhouses. (Kenneth Jessen)

Bill has unusual taste in cars, especially those that no longer run. He has positioned a 1947 Studebaker beside one of his WPA outhouses creating a unique work of art. It is not the type of art that would be sanctioned in other, less creative Colorado towns.

On July 4, the Soux hold a chicken fly. It involves paying a fee to rent a chicken. A brief time is allowed to bond with the bird.

Bill Soux holds Guffey's mayor, Monster, the black cat that greets anyone who stops and is warm and friendly. Soux's collection of outhouses can be seen in the background. (Kenneth Jessen)

Interior of the Soux's WPA sanitary privy is in near perfect condition with the toilet sitting on a concrete slab and concrete riser at a 45-degree angle. The box vent, typical of this type of outhouse, rises to a horizontal vent directly behind the seat. (Kenneth Jessen)

The chickens are launched one by one from a mailbox mounted about 15 feet above the ground. A toilet plunger is used to encourage reluctant birds to exit. The winner is determined by the distance his or her fowl flutters. No chicken has ever been injured during this annual event, but after the birds mature, most have ended up on the dinner table.

Much like thoroughbred horses, only young birds raised specifically for the chicken fly are used. One year, animal rights activists from Boulder picketed the chicken fly using placards. Soux let the protest continue, knowing that he owned the only public outhouses in Guffey. After a few hours, the protesters began asking where they could go and all fingers pointed to Soux. He allowed them to use his facilities if they put their placards in the center of Guffey's main street. Protesting against someone who provides the necessary sanitary facilities is difficult. Some apologized for their behavior. Ultimately, all of the protesters gathered up their placards, got in their flower-covered Volkswagen minibuses and headed home.

South Park Outhouses
HARTSEL: UNIQUE SCHOOLHOUSE PRIVY

The privy behind the Hartsel schoolhouse has an unusual, triangular window. Historic photographs show that this unit replaced an earlier privy. (Kenneth Jessen)

One of Colorado's earliest settlers, Samuel Hartsel, worked a placer claim at Tarryall Diggings near Fairplay in 1860. After a couple of weeks, he ran out of money and turned toward herding cattle at nearby Hamilton. Hartsel began purchasing worn-out oxen that had been used to haul wagons across the prairie. He fattened the animals and sold them to local butchers. This led to a ranching business, and in 1862, Hartsel homesteaded near the South Platte River. His ranch was located along the main route running south from Fairplay.

On his property was a hot spring. Hartsel decided to develop it for travelers. He built a primitive bathhouse with wooden tubs. This led to construction of a hotel. He piped some of the healing water to his ranch house.

Hartsel started a small town consisting of a blacksmith shop, wagon repair shop, trading post and sawmill. The standard-gauge Colorado Midland laid tracks through the town site in 1887 and built a depot, section house and divided "his" and "hers" outhouse.

In 1908, Hartsel sold his town and hot springs to retire in Denver. The springs were revitalized, and a new bathhouse was constructed. Enameled tubs replaced the wooden tubs. Today, only the foundation of the bathhouse remains with one of the tubs sitting in the middle of a pond.

South Park Outhouses
SALT WORKS PRIVY

This unusual outhouse, with separate sections for men and women, sits on the Salt Works Ranch in South Park. The commercial recovery of salt from brine springs dates to 1861. (Lyle Miller)

In 1861, J. C. Fuller purchased boilers and began producing what he called "Pikes Peak Salt," using the output from brine springs north of Antero Junction. On land adjacent to Fuller's, Charles L. Hall homesteaded the Salt Works Ranch. Apparently, Fuller abandoned his salt recovery operation, and Hall took over the operation. In 1864, Hall, John Q. A. Rollins and another investor incorporated the Colorado Salt Works. The operation expanded, including construction of a 60-foot chimney and salt-processing building containing eighteen iron evaporation kettles. Only a small percentage of the salt produced was used for human consumption with most of the output shipped to smelters for chloridizing precious metal ore.

Conflicts over the ownership of the land halted production in 1869. Salt concentration was not enough to resume production, and in addition, a great deal of fuel was required for the evaporation process. Later in 1881, investors tried to make money using a deep well to bring a higher brine concentration to the surface. This operation continued until 1883. Today, the area is closed to the public and is part of a ranch still owned by the Hall family. The chimney, a landmark for many years along U.S. 285, has since collapsed.

At a distance of about 50 yards from the ranch house, the privy was certainly not very convenient given South Park's high winds and cold winter temperatures. Very unusual for a ranch, the privy has separate sections, each with its own door. On the east side used by men, there are two adult-size toilet holes. On the women's side, there a two holes for adults and one small hole for children. The privy sits on 4x4s over a plank-lined pit. The roof is shingled with its boxed soffits and fascia mitered at the corners. The building has clapboard siding made of 6-inch boards with a 1-inch overlap. Both the interior and exterior have a certain amount of trim showing a high degree of sophistication for an outhouse.

South Park Outhouses
TARRYALL SCHOOLHOUSE PRIVIES

by Cheryl Miller

Tarryall's beginnings, like most Colorado mountain towns, were based on mining. The population in 1897 reached 1,500, and its mild climate permitted mining year-round. The town was originally called Puma City. The Tarryall name was chosen when the original Park County town of Tarryall above Como was disbanded in 1907.

The setting for Tarryall and its schoolhouse is between the Tarryall Mountains and the Puma Hills looking out on the Bison, North Tarryall, McCurdy and Tarryall peaks. The simple, white clapboard schoolhouse served the educational needs of the children of Tarryall gold miners, merchants, ranchers and farmers from 1921 to 1949.

The school building, its teacherage and privies were placed on the National Register of Historic Places in 1985. It is the best example of a one-room schoolhouse in Park County due to its distinctive architecture and location on the

Tarryall schoolhouse, constructed in 1921. (Kenneth Jessen)

original site. The schoolhouse is typical of the early twentieth century with a small building in back serving as the teacherage. In addition, there are two obligatory girls' and boys' simple, wood-frame outhouses. They are more contemporary than the schoolhouse and were constructed during the 1930s by the Works Progress Administration. Privies, such as these, were an integral part of the rural school landscape.

Almost as suddenly as the town was formed, it vanished. Many circumstances led to its demise. After the ore was exhausted, the mines closed. This was followed by the Great Depression and World War II, forcing many Tarryall families to move. Some relocated to Fort Carson to support the war effort, and the population plummeted to less than 60 inhabitants.

Today, the old Tarryall schoolhouse serves as a community center. Privies are no longer in use. The site is located in Park County, 13 miles north of Lake George on Park County Road 77 just north of the junction of Park County Road 31.

WPA sanitary privies, constructed as kits during the 1930s, located behind the Tarryall schoolhouse in South Park. (Kenneth Jessen)

Summit County Outhouses
BOSTON: ATTACHED OUTHOUSE

Attached outhouse in Boston. (Kenneth Jessen)

The mining camp of Boston was once the headquarters for the Boston Mining Company, with both placer and lode mines high on a natural amphitheater in Mayflower Gulch. The area is easy to reach, and the dirt road leading to Boston starts 5.9 miles from the Copper Mountain exit on I-70 for Colorado 91. With care, an automobile can make the trip, although the road is better suited for a vehicle with high-ground clearance.

At one Boston cabin, the miners constructed the outhouse at its entrance. What it lacked in privacy it more than made up in convenience!

Summit County Outhouses
BRECKENRIDGE: ALICE MILNE PRIVY

The Alice Milne house is a historic structure owned by the Summit Historical Society and open for tours during the summer. It was constructed by John and Maggie McNamara in 1880 and subsequently enlarged and modified. Alice Milne lived in the modest home longer than anyone else. In 1885 or 1886, the outhouse was moved from the front of the home to its present location on the north side coincident with the addition of a front parlor and bedroom. The outhouse has a unique decorative vent on its east-facing side.

The only other outhouse in the town, according to members of the Summit Historical Society, is located next to a frame home now used as a business near the corner of Washington and Main.

Top: Located east of Breckenridge on Bald Mountain, this interesting privy has a Dutch door—a rare feature and maybe the only one in Colorado. The late Vern West is standing in the doorway. (Ardie Schoeninger)

Left: The outhouse at the Alice Milne home. (Kenneth Jessen)

Summit County Outhouses
DILLON: SITE NOW UNDER WATER

Taken in 1906, Dillon grew to a sizeable town. All of the buildings in this photograph were either razed or moved. (Denver Public Library)

Settlers came to the confluence of the Snake and Blue rivers and established a stagecoach stop combined with a trading post during the early 1870s. With its strategic location, the small settlement of Dillon became a transportation hub with roads leading in all directions toward Fremont Pass, Breckenridge, Kremmling and Loveland Pass. The town site was relocated several times, but in 1882 with the arrival of the Denver, South Park & Pacific, it was firmly established with a nice business district. Stores lined both sides of its main street, and there was a public outhouse for the convenience of shoppers.

In 1955, Dillon's tranquility was shattered by the Denver Water Board. They explained to residents that a large reservoir would be built that would inundate the town. Eviction notices were issued forcing everyone to vacate Dillon by April 1, 1961. All of the structures were either razed or moved. Water began to fill behind the dam in 1963, and the project was completed the following year. A new town with the same name was established at the south end of Dillon Reservoir to meet the needs of the recreation industry.

Summit County Outhouses
FRISCO: HISTORIC PARK PRIVY

Outhouse in Frisco Historic Park. (Kenneth Jessen)

Frisco's first cabin was built by a Swedish immigrant, Henry Recen. Capt. Henry Learned, a government scout, named the town by placing a sign over the door to Recen's cabins that read, "Frisco City." Although there had been placer mining in the area, Frisco burst to life in 1878 with the discovery of silver ore in Tenmile Canyon. The town got a post office a year later.

It took nearly a century to get the recording fee for the Frisco town site paid. In 1885, the patent for the land was granted to the town company, and the records were forwarded to the county seat in Breckenridge. The $5 recording fee, however, was overlooked. The bill was lost until 1924 when it was mailed to the Frisco postmaster. He filed it with his personal papers, and it wasn't discovered until 1979 by his son. The $5 recording fee was finally paid.

There are several ways to preserve history. With the advent of the ski industry, development pressure threatened Frisco's historic structures. Centered on the schoolhouse, a historic park was established in 1983, and many of the old log and frame structures were moved to the site. The Frisco Historic Park contains a variety of early day structures, including a schoolhouse, log chapel and a number of homes.

Summit County Outhouses

LINCOLN CITY: STEEL OUTHOUSE

Prospectors resentful of Harry Farncomb waged a war to take away his rich mining property along French Creek east of Breckenridge. The war started in the courts and escalated into a seven-hour gun battle leaving three dead.

Lincoln City was founded in 1861 at the time of the "war." It got its post office that year, and the post office remained open until 1894 when the town was all but abandoned.

Only a few buildings are left today, but at its peak, Lincoln City had a store, two hotels, seven smelters plus a stamp mill.

Steel-sided outhouse at Lincoln City along French Creek east of Breckenridge. (Kenneth Jessen)

Examples of the few buildings left at Lincoln City. (Kenneth Jessen)

Summit County Outhouses
MONTEZUMA'S REVENGE

Montezuma, located in Summit County not far from the Keystone Ski Resort, has a "his" and "hers" outhouse sitting in the central portion of town on a vacant lot. Fire destroyed many of Montezuma's commercial buildings, including the one that stood on this lot, but the privy was spared.

The town was named by an early prospector for the famous Aztec emperor. The first store opened in 1866, and the town continued

Old outhouse in the middle of Montezuma in Summit County. (Kenneth Jessen)

to grow until silver prices began their decline during the 1880s culminating when the United States abandoned the silver standard in 1893. For decades, Montezuma was partially abandoned, however, recent trends in the development of recreation in Summit County have spurred reoccupation of the town.

Summit County Outhouses

PENNSYLVANIA MILL AND PERU CREEK

The nearby town of Decatur was wiped off the map by successive avalanches leaving only foundation platforms dug into the hillside. On the opposite side of the valley stands the Pennsylvania Mill, but it will not be long until it is a pile of jumbled wood and metal. A collapsed outhouse sits between the mill and the stone foundations of the boarding house.

Pennsylvania Mill on Peru Creek is one of few wood-frame mills left standing in Colorado. (Kenneth Jessen)

Cabins dot the landscape along Peru Creek. Mining began in the late 1870s and continued at a fast pace until the price of silver began to drop at the end of the nineteenth century. Only the best mines survived into the twentieth century, and today, there are only the sounds of the creek, birds and occasional visitors.

The window in an abandoned cabin frames this outhouse sitting in the lush meadow along Peru Creek. (Ardie Schoeninger)

Summit County Outhouses
SLATE CREEK HALL VENTILATED PRIVIES

The unincorporated ranching village of Slate Creek was located 12 miles north of Silverthorne east of Colorado 9 on FR 1450.

The Slate Creek Hall and its "his" and "hers" twin outhouses remain standing. The structures were built by local ranchers in 1936 as part of a WPA project. The privies have exceptionally nice proportions incorporating double louvered vents on the side. According to Summit County historian Mary Ellen Gilliland, nearby the Slate Creek Hall once stood a cook shed, combination feed store and residence plus a small home. Still standing is a log schoolhouse constructed in the 1890s and a teacherage. The community also had a saloon, now collapsed.

Outhouses behind Slate Creek Hall north of Silverthorne. (Kenneth Jessen)

Summit County Outhouses

WAPITI: EXTRA TALL OUTHOUSE

Wapiti is located above the former county seat of Parkville on a road connecting the Swan River drainage with French Creek in Summit County. Its location near Farncomb Hill placed it in one of the richest mineralized areas in Colorado. The town consisted of this outhouse, a combination store and living

Outhouse at Wapiti, and partially collapsed store at Wapiti in Summit County. (Kenneth Jessen)

quarters plus several cabins. A four-wheel drive vehicle is best suited to reach the site.

Wapiti was originally named Victoria, and for reasons unknown, the name was changed in 1894 coincident with the establishment of a post office. The partially collapsed combination store and living quarters is interesting in that the front half is a frame structure while the back half is made of logs.

The outhouse at Wapiti sits on a hillside behind the store building and has a walkway to the entrance. The privy is surrounded by discarded cans.

Teller County Outhouses
AMERICAN EAGLES MINE

The American Eagles Mine is open to the public and can be reached by a graded dirt road from Victor. It is operated as an outdoor museum by the Victor and Cripple Creek Gold Mining Company. This mine has one of the highest elevations in the Cripple Creek/Victor District at over 10,400 feet and was purchased in 1895 by millionaire William S. Stratton. By 1902, its shaft had reached a depth of 1,540 feet making it the deepest shaft in the area. The mine was worked intermittently, then in 1936, a rich pocket of ore was discovered. An attached outhouse served the mine office. The mine operated until 1940.

American Eagles Mine office and attached privy. (Kenneth Jessen)

Teller County Outhouses
ANACONDA: FALLEN OUTHOUSE

It is sad to see a fallen outhouse such as this one near Anaconda Mine's blacksmith shop between Victor and Cripple Creek. (Kenneth Jessen)

Anaconda burned to the ground in November 1904, and the town was never rebuilt. The only structures that survived were high above the original town site, including a blacksmith shop, its privy and several homes.

Typical of so many Colorado mining towns, Anaconda went through a number of name changes. A prospector came across the remains of an Indian woman and named the shallow canyon Squaw Gulch. A mining camp by the same name was formed. In 1892, Vinton and Bill Barry laid out a town that included the existing buildings in Squaw Gulch and named the place Barry. The Barry brothers purchased the Anaconda Mine at the head of the gulch, and in 1894, the town of Barry was renamed Anaconda. The town itself consisted of a long row of buildings in Squaw Gulch that stretched toward another mining camp called Mound City.

Teller County Outhouses
GOLDFIELD: VARIED OUTHOUSES

A stone outhouse once served residents of a home in Goldfield. (Kenneth Jessen)

Goldfield was known as the "City of Homes," a family town with schools and churches. It was founded by the owners of the nearby Portland Mine in 1895, and a year later, its population exceeded 2,000. It was laid out in a large meadow only a short distance from Victor at an elevation of nearly 10,000 feet. The town was served by three railroads, including an electric trolley line running through the town and curving around the hillside.

Today, the town is almost abandoned with only a handful of residents living among its vacant lots and dilapidated abandoned buildings. But, it does have character.

When an outhouse pit is filled to dangerous levels, wood-frame outhouses can be picked up or slid to a new pit. When an outhouse is made of stone or brick, the pit has to be emptied by hand, an unpleasant thought. Goldfield's substantial stone outhouse sits on private property and is definitely not portable. Stone outhouses are rare.

Wood-frame outhouses are more common, and one nicely proportioned outhouse is located in the lower portion of town. It remains in use and is located on private property. Plans are included in case the reader wishes to duplicate this structure (next page).

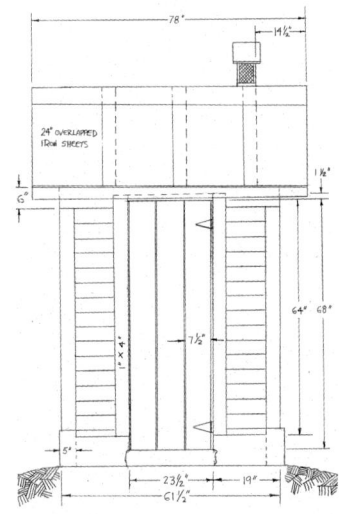

A shake shingle roof is used in place of a roof made of overlapping iron sheets in this scale model. (Kenneth Jessen)

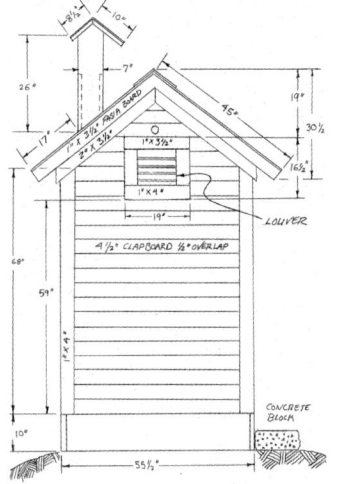

This nicely proportioned outhouse sits in the lower portion of Goldfield on private property. Plans for this structure are shown here. (Kenneth Jessen)

Teller County Outhouses
THERESA MINE PRIVY REQUIRED COURAGE

Unlike flush toilets, when an outhouse pit is full, the structure has to either be moved or the pit has to be emptied. If, however, the pit is extremely deep, then the problem is eliminated, and a mineshaft meets this qualification. The outhouse at the Theresa Mine near Goldfield is located over an abandoned mineshaft. To use this privy and walk across the planks looking down into the dark abyss between the planks takes courage and a sense of urgency.

The Theresa Gold Mining Company worked this mine from 1895 to 1900. From that point on, it was opened to lessees and continued production until 1961.

The Theresa Mine near Goldfield is accessible to the public, thanks to a new walking trail.

Theresa Mine headframe near Goldfield (Kenneth Jessen)

An open mine shaft serves as the pit for the Theresa Mine outhouse. Planks supporting the structure are rotting away, and this outhouse eventually will fall into to the deposits made over the years. (Kenneth Jessen)

Teller County Outhouses
VICTOR: DECORATIVE TIN PRIVY

Trimmed with elaborate pressed tin siding, this outhouse in Victor is divided into small rooms. Only the center section served as a toilet, while small rooms to either side were used for storage of coal or firewood. (Kenneth Jessen)

An elaborate outhouse decorated with pressed tin siding sits along one of Victor's side streets. In the center of this structure are stairs leading to a small porch.

In 1893, Frank and Harry Woods paid $1,000 for a 136-acre placer claim and laid out the town of Victor. The Woods brothers named the town for Victor Adams, one of the original homesteaders at the nearby community of Lawrence.

Since Victor was built on a placer claim, the Woods brothers spread the word that every lot had the potential of becoming a gold mine. This turned out to be true for Frank Woods when he was digging the foundation for a hotel. He struck a 20-inch vein of rich, gold ore and sunk a shaft. He named it the Gold Coin, and it brought in a respectable $50,000 a month.

Victor's most famous citizen was news correspondent Lowell Thomas. Thomas graduated from high school in Victor, and after receiving his education, worked as a newspaper editor for one of the town's publications. He moved away to become a leading newspaper columnist and eventually the first television news anchor. His career spanned more than four decades.

Upper Arkansas Valley Outhouses
CAMP CREE: MASSIVE LOG PRIVY

The outhouse at Camp Cree, at the head of Cree Creek in Chaffee County, certainly qualifies as one of the most massive structures of its type in Colorado. The cabins that constitute this mining camp are spread out in two shallow valleys at timberline. The site can be reached by a four-wheel drive road from U.S. 50 on the east side of Monarch Pass.

Massive log outhouse at Camp Cree near Monarch Pass. (Kenneth Jessen)

Upper Arkansas Valley Outhouses

CRYSTAL LAKES SCHOOLHOUSE PRIVY

South of Leadville along U.S. 24 at the parking lot for Crystal Lakes is an old schoolhouse constructed in 1884. Behind the schoolhouse and just below U.S. 24 is a boys' and girls' outhouse with a wing in the back for coal storage. The coal storage room has its own door on the front of the privy.

During the nineteenth century, Hugh Young, a local rancher, ran the Crystal Lakes House near the site. It was a resort served by the Denver & Rio Grande Railway.

Crystal Lakes schoolhouse and outhouse with separate boys' and girls' toilets and a coal storage room. Far left: the spartan interior of the outhouse. (Kenneth Jessen)

Upper Arkansas Valley Outhouses
DERRY RANCH AND ITS VIOLENT PAST

The Derry Ranch is listed on the National Register of Historic Places. It is one of Colorado's most unusual ghost towns. Samuel Derry patented the shallow valley east of Mount Elbert along Corske and Box creeks in 1878. His ranch yielded hay for the numerous draft animals working the mines in the upper Arkansas River drainage.

The following year, Warren Hussey and Gen. Horatio B. Bearce, a Denver businessman, formed a placer mining company to remove the free gold from the gravel in this broad valley. The placer mining was done west of Derry's ranch between the headgate to his water supply and his ranch. This contaminated the water with silt flowing into Derry's property. Consequently, Derry sought legal action to prevent further mining on the placer. Hussey and Bearce offered to purchase Derry's ranch, but Derry refused to sell because raising hay was quite lucrative.

On June 7, 1884, after two years of inactivity, Bearce and a party of men entered the deposit. Their purpose was

Three cabins constructed in 1916 for the dredge workers. (Kenneth Jessen)

Collapsed outhouse at the Derry Ranch near dredge workers' cabins, probably constructed in 1916. (Kenneth Jessen)

to make a survey. Derry approached them and told them they were trespassing on his land. Bearce called the 66-year-old Derry a liar. Derry raised a shovel to threaten Bearce but fell over backward into a ditch. Derry retreated to his ranch house, but later that afternoon, confronted Bearce and his men again as they passed by his home. Derry asked Bearce, "So you think I have perjured myself?" To this, the General agreed and was promptly shot by Derry. Bearce died of his wound a day and a half later, and Derry voluntarily surrendered to the sheriff.

The people in Leadville were outraged by this senseless murder of a prominent businessman. The trial followed in December and captivated Leadville residents. A plea of temporary insanity was entered on behalf of Derry. Witnesses told of a crazy uncle and erratic behavior, abuse of his family and fits of rage. Leadville's citizens were astonished when Derry was acquitted.

Derry passed away in 1889 from burns suffered in a fall into the fireplace. His son operated the ranch until his death in 1908. At that time, a gold-mining company purchased the property and resumed mining. In 1913, the land was purchased by the New York Engineering Company, and in 1916, a large dredge was erected on the site. At this time, a number of log cabins were constructed near the ranch house for the men working on the dredge.

After it became uneconomical to recover gold in Corske Creek, the dredge was sold and moved to nearby Box Creek and continued to operate until 1926. The Derry Ranch was abandoned with the exception of 1935 to 1937, when it was occupied by renters.

Upper Arkansas Valley Outhouses

FINNTOWN: ONCE HAD A SIX-SIDED, CORRUGATED STEEL PRIVY

Located immediately east of Leadville in Stray Horse Gulch was one of many satellite-mining camps. Finntown was occupied first by immigrants from Cleator Moor, England. The place was originally called Cleator Moor. But after its English residents moved on, the town became predominately Finnish and Swedish in ethic origin, and its name became Finntown.

The buildings were mostly corrugated steel sheets nailed over a lumber frame. In 1941, Muriel Sibell Wolle, author of the classic, *Stampede to Timberline*, photographed Finntown, including an unusual, six-sided outhouse. It sat off by itself away from other structures. Windows admitted light, and the roof was faceted and topped with a decorative ball. Also unusual was the arched doorway with ornamental brackets on either side. This structure has long disappeared, however, there are still a few buildings at Finntown.

Ghost town historian Muriel Sibell Wolle photographed this six-sided outhouse in Finntown in 1941. (Denver Public Library)

Upper Arkansas Valley Outhouses
FUTURITY

L ocated in a high meadow between Turret and Trout Creek Pass, Futurity is among the most obscure mining camps in Colorado. Many of its original cabins remain standing and are seasonally occupied. Miners had to walk only 100 feet or so to work since the mine sits almost in the middle of town. The geology of the area is similar to Turret to the south with pockets of gold ore in a granite formation.

Current residents have posted a number of humorous signs on their cabins. Lacking indoor plumbing, outhouses are widely used.

A plywood box supports the toilet seat in this Futurity outhouse in Bassum Park south of Trout Creek Pass. (Ardie Schoeninger)

One of several humorous signs posted on the buildings in Futurity. (Ardie Schoeninger)

Upper Arkansas Valley Outhouses
GRANITE: MODIFIED WPA SANITARY PRIVIES

Established in 1867, Granite was one of the first towns along the upper Arkansas River. It was founded on mining and milling, and in 1868, it became the Lake County seat. It took this position away from Dayton (now called Twin Lakes) by popular vote. In 1879, in response to the rapidly growing population of Leadville, Lake County was formed, and Leadville was named the new county seat. Granite became the Chaffee County seat. A year later, the county seat was moved to Buena Vista as Granite began to fade.

Top: This propped up outhouse sits behind an old log home that has undergone extensive restoration in Granite. (Kenneth Jessen)

Left: Modified WPA sanitary privies at Granite schoolhouse. (Benjamin Jessen)

Upper Arkansas Valley Outhouses
INTER-LAKEN: HEXAGONAL OUTHOUSE

The now deserted buildings at Inter-Laken were once part of a popular mountain resort started in 1879 by John A. Staley. The site sits on the south shore where the two lakes that constitute Twin Lakes Reservoir join. It remained a small resort until millionaire James V. Dexter purchased the property in 1883 and gave it the name Inter-Laken.

In 1893, Dexter constructed an elaborate summer home on the site and continued to develop the resort. Business began to decline in 1897 when a reservoir company constructed a dam on the lower lake raising the water level. The primary access to Inter-Laken across the stream between the two lakes was inundated along with the road along the south shore. Although the road was rebuilt on higher ground, the resort did not turn a profit. After Dexter's death in 1899, the hotel was relegated to a boardinghouse. After World War I, the buildings were abandoned.

Under Dexter's ownership, the front side of the log hotel was covered with siding. On the second floor, there was a two-seat privy over a shaft leading to a cesspool. To

Hexagonal outhouse that once served guests at the Inter-Laken Hotel annex. Toilet seats were covered in leather. (Kenneth Jessen)

accommodate an increase in business, an annex was constructed. Within the annex, each door was lettered. To serve guests staying in the annex, a hexagonal outhouse was constructed. The outhouse was equipped with private stalls, each with a letter of the alphabet on the door. The letters corresponded to the letters on the rooms within the annex. In keeping with the times, women stayed in the main hotel building, and male guests stayed in the annex.

Inter-Laken was added to the National Register of Historic Places in 1974, including its unusual outhouse.

Coincident with the construction of a new and higher dam at the lower lake, the Inter-Laken Hotel, Dexter's home and some of the buildings were moved to higher ground in 1980. The buildings were set on sturdy foundations, stabilized structurally and painted. The hexagonal outhouse had fallen over and was set upright on a new foundation. The U. S. Forest Service has added an extensive set of interpretive signs that explain Inter-Laken's history. The Inter-Laken Hotel is located along the Colorado Trail on the south shore of Twin Lakes.

Inter-Laken Hotel. (Kenneth Jessen)

Upper Arkansas Valley Outhouses

LEADVILLE: OUTHOUSE RACE

Leadville's outhouse race down Harrison Avenue during Boom Days is something that any outhouse aficionado must experience. (Kenneth Jessen)

At 10,200 feet, oxygen depravation may play a role in outhouse racing during Leadville's Boom Days. At the beginning of the second day is the start of the men's burro race up Mosquito Pass reaching an elevation of 13,183 feet and covering a distance of 21 miles. The little, four-legged animals know they are about to be pulled and prodded over rough trails at a dead run and lightened their load on Harrison Avenue.

To kick things off, a gunfight is staged in the center of Harrison Avenue. At noon, after a minimal amount of clean up, there is "The Mosey," where families walk 100 yards down Harrison Avenue in their nineteenth-century period clothing, followed by the outhouse race. The same outhouse is used by each team, and one team member must ride inside. The outhouse has been modified with casters, and to make it street legal, sports a Colorado license plate. The idea is for two team members to pull using ropes, while two push. At the starting gun, the outhouse is propelled down the street, around a set of cones and back to the start/finish line. Despite tricky footing, thanks to the burros, impressive times are achieved.

Upper Arkansas Valley Outhouses
MALTA SCHOOL OUTHOUSE

Malta is approximately 2.5 miles south of Leadville on U.S. 24. It is marked by its schoolhouse and outhouse that date to 1882. Smelters were essential to the mining industry for the recovery of precious metals—lead and zinc from the complex ore found in the Leadville area. Malta became a smelter town, and by 1876, the population grew to 150.

Malta was not the town's original name, however. It was originally called Galena, but apparently the name lacked originality. Since one of the major investors was named Swill, the name Swilltown was suggested. This name carried a negative connotation that the place was filled with drunks, and the idea was dropped. The first smelter was constructed by the Malta Smelting and Mining Company, and the people decided to take the smelter's name.

The town had two grocery stores, one of them operated by H. A. W. Tabor, who would become one of Colorado's wealthiest men. The post office opened in 1875 and closed in 1887 as other smelters closer to Leadville began to take away business. With renewed business and improvements in the town's smelter, Malta's population increased, and the post office reopened in 1890 and remained opened until 1950.

Malta schoolhouse and half-moon privy. (Kenneth Jessen)

Upper Arkansas Valley Outhouses

MARY MURPHY MINE: DEPOSITORS HAD TO WALK THE PLANK

The outhouse at the Mary Murphy Mine sits near a small creek running through the site. The pit is shallow due to the difficulty digging into the rocky hillside.

During the 1870s, the ore body at this site was discovered by Dr. A. E. Wright and John Royal. Mary Murphy was a Denver nurse who cared for John Royal and nursed him back to health. For her kindness, he named the mine in her honor. The Mary Murphy was the largest mine in Chalk Creek Canyon, and the site is located in Pomeroy Gulch above Romley and not far from St. Elmo.

Rocky soil limited the depth of the outhouse pit behind the Mary Murphy mine office. (Kenneth Jessen)

This outhouse sits over the edge of mine tailings at the Tressie C Mine, over the ridge from the Mary Murphy Mine. (Cyndi Trombly)

Upper Arkansas Valley Outhouses
ORO CITY: HOME OF H.A.W. TABOR

Gold was the first precious metal discovered in the Leadville area. Extensive placer deposits were found in California Gulch, and a mining camp called Oro City was formed up and down the gulch. Although there were a few business buildings, most of the camp was composed of shanties located haphazardly near the stream.

In May 1860, Horace Austin Warner Tabor and his first wife, Augusta, arrived in Oro City. The Tabors slaughtered their only oxen and divided the meat among the miners, thus preventing mass starvation. They operated a small store at the future site of Leadville. Tabor went on to become one of the wealthiest men in Colorado and to cheat on his wife. He divorced Augusta and married his mistress, Baby Doe. After a lavish life, Tabor lost his millions and died in poverty.

An interesting photograph inscribed "Frist <sic> Miner's Cabin in California Gulch where Millions in gold was taken out" appears in Denver Public Library's collection. The terrain in the background resembles the land near the mouth of California Gulch. The outhouse located near the primitive cabin looks newer and in better condition than the cabin itself. This could have been the home of Abe Lee, credited with constructing the first cabin in the area using money he made acting as the recorder for new mining claims.

The inscription on this photograph indicates that this is the first cabin constructed in California Gulch. Note the outhouse seems in better shape than the cabin. (Denver Public Library)

Upper Arkansas Valley Outhouses

ST. ELMO: COLORADO'S POPULAR GHOST TOWN

Outhouses at the end of St. Elmo's main street do not look like they have been used for many years. (Kenneth Jessen)

One of Colorado's most popular ghost towns was originally called Forest City. It was founded, in part, because of the rich ore at the nearby Mary Murphy Mine. There was a Forest City, California, and because of potential confusion, the U.S. Postal Service requested that the name of the town be changed. A committee selected St. Elmo, the title of a novel by Augusta J. Evans, as the town's new name.

After the ore was exhausted and the local mining industry died, St. Elmo was nearly abandoned. By 1926, only a half-dozen people remained in a town that once supported a population of more than 500.

Today, many of the cabins have been restored for seasonal use, and there is a general store in operation. Most of the abandoned buildings along the town's main street have been preserved and stabilized.

Upper Arkansas Valley Outhouses

TURRET: NO UNINVITED DEPOSITORS

There is an outhouse with a corrugated sheet metal roof located between large boulders in the town of Turret. The padlock on the door indicates that its owner does not want uninvited visitors to use the facility.

Vivandiere Mine near Turret. Note the wooden water tank, mine buildings and outhouse on the right. (Denver Public Library)

Padlocked outhouse in Turret. (Keith Maull)

Turret began in 1884 when David Austin moved his timber-cutting operation up Cat Gulch and constructed several small cabins called Camp Austin. After gold was discovered, the name was changed to Turret. Unfortunately, Turret has been subdivided recently and is being developed as a mountain community. Possibly the new arrivals do not know of the town's historic significance since many of its old buildings are being cleared away.

The Vivandiere Mine was located 1 mile east of Turret at the head of Cat Gulch. Gold ore with a high copper content was discovered, and mining began in 1900. By 1910, all hope of making a profit had vanished. To recover $70,000 in gold, an estimated quarter of a million dollars was spent on the mine.

Upper Arkansas Valley Outhouses

TWIN LAKES: FORMERLY CALLED DAYTON

Twin Lakes outhouse in 1982. Note door is blocked by a board. (Ardie Schoeninger)

Oro City, near Leadville, was once the largest population center in Lake County and was named the county seat in 1861 by the Colorado Territorial Legislature. Enough votes were mustered, however, by the voters in Dayton to move the county seat in 1866. The prominence of Dayton, however, was short-lived, and it lost the county seat to Granite in 1868.

Dayton was abandoned and was even referred to as "Deserted Village." It was rediscovered by tourists, and its virtues as a summer resort were extolled by the media. Cool summer evenings and its proximity to Twin Lakes made it ideal. In 1879, Dayton was reborn as Twin Lakes when a new post office opened. In 1881, a toll road was completed through Twin Lakes over Independence Pass to Aspen and put the town on a major trade route.

Most of the homes in Twin Lakes are seasonally occupied and many of its outhouses remain in use.

chapter 5

OUTHOUSES OF

SOUTH-CENTRAL COLORADO

Coal Camp Privies
COKEDALE: COAL SHEDS

Cokedale privies were built by the American Smelting and Refining Company in 1906-1907, according to standardized plans. (Kenneth Jessen)

Most Colorado coal towns were constructed by Colorado Fuel & Iron. Cokedale, located west of Trinidad in Las Animas County, is an exception. It was built by the American Smelting and Refining Company in 1906-1907. By 1909, its population grew to 1,500. There were two mines that supported the town along with 350 coke ovens. The town was served by the Colorado & Wyoming Railroad and had daily service to Trinidad.

Most of the area's coal-mining towns lasted only until the 1920s, but Cokedale hung on. In 1947, American Smelting and Refining Company announced that the town would be closed and sold for its scrap value to the Florence Machinery Company. The company offered the families living in Cokedale the chance to buy their homes. The price was $450, including the land. The town was incorporated in 1948 by its residents and survives today as one of the only examples of an intact coal camp. In 1984, it was listed on the National Register of Historic Places along with the 350 coke ovens located south of the town site.

Any Cokedale alley appears to be a privy aficionado's dream come true. Structures straddle each property line with two rooms separated by a stout plank wall. There are doors on opposite ends to serve each home. Upon close examination, however, the interior has a plank floor and no bench for toilet seats. Small, square doors next to the roof face the alley. These are not outhouses, but coal sheds. All are identical and were built by American Smelting and Refining Company as part of company housing. There are outhouses in Cokedale, many with similar architectural features as the coal sheds.

Coal sheds, not privies, straddling the property lines in Cokedale. (Kenneth Jessen)

Coal Camp Privies
ENGLEVILLE: WPA SANITARY PRIVY ON RAILS

This WPA Sanitary Privy retains its concrete slab and concrete riser supporting the toilet seat. The seat and vents are also original. Note structure rests on two rails to keep it from falling into the pit. (F. Dean Sneed)

Southeast of Trinidad is the abandoned, coal-mining town of Engleville (sometimes called Engle) in Las Animas County. It is one of the oldest camps in the area and was originally owned by the Colorado Coal & Iron Company. Its post office opened in 1882 and lasted until 1913. In 1892, Colorado Coal & Iron Company became part of Colorado Fuel & Iron. The town was named for George Engle, the first mine superintendent.

Italians dominated the ethnic groups in Engleville with some Mexicans and people of Slavic origin. Few residents were born in the United States, according to Colorado Fuel & Iron records. By 1902, Engleville reached an estimated population of 1,000.

Engleville has a number of abandoned buildings and a small cemetery, but it is all on private property. Permission to enter the site must be obtained.

Coal Camp Privies
HASTINGS

Based on photographs, Hastings, a Victor-American Fuel Company town, lacked the neat appearance of a comparable Colorado Fuel & Iron towns. A half-dozen shack-like outhouses are in the foreground. All structures are now gone. (Family Album Photographers, Trinidad)

Not all of Colorado's coal-mining camps were owned and operated by Colorado Fuel & Iron. Hastings was a Victor-American Fuel Company town in Las Animas County. The site is located west of Ludlow in Canyon del Agua.

Hastings was established in 1889 and grew to an estimated population of 3,000, with a business district consisting of stores, hotel, barbershops and many saloons. The town had a Catholic Church and a public school.

Hastings is not remembered so much for its size, its coke ovens or the output from its mine as much as the mine disaster that occurred on April 27, 1917. Evidence shows that a mine inspector, responsible for the safety of others, caused the explosion. When his safety lamp went out, he accidentally ignited explosive gas in an attempt to re-light the lamp. The explosion killed 121 miners. Many died, not from the concussion, but from the poisonous gas created by the blast.

The portals of the Hastings Mine were sealed in 1923. Except for a small monument to the miners that died and a row of crumbing coke ovens, little remains at the site.

Coal Camp Privies
LUDLOW MASSACRE SITE

A WPA Sanitary Privy sits near abandoned homes in Ludlow, located north of Trinidad. (Ardie Schoeninger)

Along its dusty main street are the abandoned remains of Ludlow's business district, and to the south are several abandoned homes. This is all that is left of Ludlow, and if it were not the site of a massacre, it would be just another deserted coal-mining town. The massacre took place on April 20, 1914, during a bitter strike for better working conditions. During the course of the strike, the coal companies evicted the miners and their families from the company-owned cottages, forcing them to set up a tent city at Ludlow. As more families were evicted, the camp swelled to more than 1,000 people in an estimated 275 tents.

As the situation grew worse and acts of violence on both sides increased, the Colorado National Guard was summoned. Under fire, the guardsmen poured hundreds of rounds into the tent camp as men, women and children took shelter in pits dug below the tents. Ruthless strikebreakers brought in by the mine owners encouraged the guardsmen to use their machine guns to suppress any gunfire by the miners in the tent camp. After the shooting stopped, guardsmen used coal oil to ignite the tents. Women and children suffocated. In all, eighteen miners and their families were killed in this event, the worst in Colorado history. Their names are inscribed on a monument south of the town site. The monument sits over one of the pits where eleven children and two women suffocated.

Coal Camp Privies
REDSTONE

Redstone, in Pitkin County, is a wonderful, well-maintained mountain town with Swiss-German architecture. It has several restaurants, an inn, art galleries and general store. Its structures are part of a historic district listed on the National Register of Historic Places. The town was founded by John C. Osgood, who purchased a nearby coal deposit in Coalbasin. He organized the Colorado Coal Company in 1887 to develop the deposit. His company was later combined with Colorado Iron to form the giant Colorado Fuel & Iron Company. Osgood headed C.F.&I. from 1892 to 1903, and it grew to become Colorado's largest industry.

At Redstone, coke ovens were constructed along with company housing. This included an elaborate clubhouse with billiard and pool tables, card room, library, reading room, showers and dressing rooms. Osgood also built a large mansion he called Cleveholm.

Influenced by Osgood's care for his workers, eighty-four cottages were constructed. To avoid the monotony typical of other company towns, houses of different sizes were mixed, and each painted a different color. Many of these structures remain today.

Ron Thompson moved this privy onto a pad and restored it to match his home. It now serves as a tool shed. (Kenneth Jessen)

Coal Camp Privies
ROCKVALE

This interesting corrugated steel outhouse is among several similar structures in Rockvale. (Kenneth Jessen)

Col. William Horace May homesteaded southwest of Florence in 1863 in what is now Fremont County. Coal was discovered on May's property, and Benjamin Rockafellow, with several Canon City businessmen, leased the deposit. A coal company was formed with May serving as one of its directors. A town was founded on the May homestead to house the miners, and it took the name Rockvale for Benjamin Rockafellow.

The town and coal deposits were purchased by Colorado Fuel & Iron. Typical of other C.F.&I. towns, company cottages were constructed, adding to the homes already in Rockvale. During a coal-miners' strike in 1927, C.F.&I. told the miners that unless they got back to work, they would shut off the pumps and allow the mine to flood. This they did, and Rockvale began a steady decline.

Today, the Rockvale schoolhouse stands with a modern, cinder block vaulted outhouse in back. Along its side streets are other interesting privies of varying design.

Coal Camp Privies
TOLLERBURG: PRIVIES THAT COULD BE CLEANED

Tollerburg, in Road Canyon. Its privies can be seen between the buildings. (Denver Public Library)

Road Canyon west of Ludlow is filled with the remains of mines and buildings. Today, there are crumbling walls, stairs leading to nowhere and extensive rows of foundations spread out for more than 4 miles. Road Canyon was once home to a considerable population of miners. Cedar Hill sat at the entrance to Road Canyon followed by Tabasco a half-mile up the road. Berwind was next, then Tollerburg, and finally Vallorso.

Tollerburg was originally developed by a local businessman and landowner, Giacomo Toller, according to historian F. Dean Sneed in his excellent book, *Las Animas County Ghost Towns and Mining Camps*. The town and its mines were soon leased to the Cedar Hill Coal & Coke Company. Tollerburg had a general merchandise store and saloon, livery stable, barber shop, hotel, school, YMCA and a number of company-built

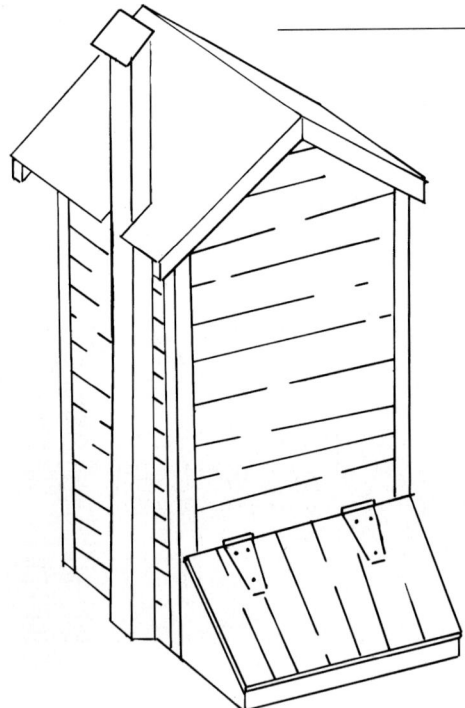

A door in the back of each privy allowed waste products to be removed as necessary.

cottages. Shortly after World War I, Colorado Fuel & Iron purchased the entire operation, and mining continued until 1932. At that time, Tollerburg was abandoned, and according to C.F.&I. policy, the buildings were moved or razed.

It is difficult to say who designed and built the standard privy in Tollerburg, but it was probably C.F.&I. The back of each privy had a large, hinged door to allow removal of waste products. By each privy was a coal bin. An alley provided access so that coal could be delivered and waste products in privies mucked out as necessary.

Coal Camp Privies
VALDEZ

Valdez, in Las Animas County, is located 11 miles west of Trinidad and a short distance south of Colorado 12 on a side road. It was named for Gabriel Valdez, a homesteader. During its peak in the early part of the twentieth century, it reached a population of around 1,500. There were stores, combination hotel and boardinghouse, restaurant, two schools plus many homes.

The Frederick Mine, operated by Colorado Fuel & Iron, supported the town. Among the longest-lived mines along the Purgatoire River, it produced coal for 53 years. After the mine's closure in 1961, Valdez lost much of its population. Today, several of its structures remain standing, and some are being restored.

Along the main street of Valdez is an outhouse on the verge of collapse. (F. Dean Sneed)

Coal Camp Privies
VALLORSO

Outhouses at Vallorso. According to F. Dean Sneed, author of *Las Animas County Ghost Towns and Mining Camps*, the outhouse on the right has collapsed since this photograph was taken and only a pile of wood remains. (Ardie Schoeninger)

Vallorso, about 6 miles west of Ludlow, was the highest coal-mining town in Road Canyon and was the terminus of the Colorado & Southern's spur serving these camps. Established in 1918, its economy depended on three mines close to the town. In the same year, Vallorso got its own post office. The most successful area mine was the Bear Canyon, but it was plagued by a succession of gas explosions and floods. It closed in 1953, and Vallorso was abandoned a year later.

OLD-TIME OUTHOUSE IS GOING THE WAY OF ALL FLUSH
by Ed Quillen

Ed Quillen lives in Salida and writes two columns a week for the *Denver Post*. He is also publisher of *Colorado Central*.

Twin men's and women's privy once served passengers waiting at the Denver, South Park & Pacific depot in Pitkin. (Benjamin Jessen)

Few structures exemplify the rural landscape so much as the humble privy. It is a symbol of human occupation but also a stark reminder that we haven't really conquered the privy's domain. If dams, diversion tunnels, treatment plants, and various other facets of hot-and-cold running civilization were all present, then the privy wouldn't be.

Despite this impressive absence of any need for expensive infrastructure, the traditional privy, an outhouse over an unlined pit, is a strong candidate for the endangered-structures list.

For one thing, development works against it. Custer County in the Wet Mountain Valley of Colorado held only 1,296 people in 1990. Most lived in town, and the rest, scattered on ranches, were so dispersed that their outhouses could produce no discernible effect on distant neighbors' drinking water.

This little booklet was produced by the Friends of the Jackson County Library in Walden as a fund-raiser. (Kenneth Jessen)

But the neighbors aren't so distant now. At the Census Bureau's reckoning a year ago, Custer had 3,062 residents, making it the fourth-fastest-growing county in the nation. Many of those new people have bought into 35-acre ranchettes, which puts one's well way too close to the neighbor's coliform-generating outhouse.

The county had little choice but to outlaw the old privies. As of Dec. 31 (1997), all must be closed. Those without running water can go with chemical toilets or vaults that must be pumped.

Nor is the old-time privy a feature of public land. Those outhouses at Forest Service and BLM campgrounds sit over vaults, and that's been the case since the 1960s.

"We're very concerned about stream pollution," explained Anne Ewing, forestry technician at the local Forest Service office, who added: "I take my toilets seriously."

So seriously that she's trying to develop an architectural history of one old-timer at the Monarch Park campground. "It's a very solid structure," she said, "and we think it was built by the Civilian Conservation Corps back in the 1930s. But we haven't found the records."

Apparently it wasn't as well-documented as the $330,000 outhouse—vaulted, of course—that the National Park Service just built in Pennsylvania.

But the main evidence that the genuine privy is vanishing is that the necessity of yesteryear has become quaint and cute, worthy of special attention like a steam locomotive or soda fountain.

In Walden, the library conducted a privy tour last year as a fundraiser. Some marketing material from Crested Butte brags that the town gets so much snow that it used to need two-story privies. Upscale gardeners now bid on abandoned privies, hoping to restore them into picturesque tool sheds. One local bookstore offers the 1998 "Outhouses" calendar, with spectacular color photography of privies in the desert, on the beach, and, of course, among soaring peaks and verdant meadows. None appeared as scenic as a friend's privy, close to town but not yet discovered by the county sanitary enforcement squad. It has but half a door, thus allowing unhurried contemplation of the Sangre de Cristo Mountains rising majestically from the Arkansas River and stretching southward to Santa Fe.

Nor were any calendar outhouses as exquisitely weathered as the first one I remember at my grandfather's ranch between Bill and Dull Center in Wyoming. (Bill's population was really nine people, we used to joke—the one fellow who ran the general store and post office, and the inhabitants of the two buildings in back, one "4 women" and the other "4 men.") A .410 shotgun hung over the door of the ranch house, for killing rattlers on the way to the outhouse where one did not tarry, since its splintered knothole walls were adored with wasp nests.

But I loved it when I was a little kid—I thought Grandpa

Pump house west of Loveland. (Kenneth Jessen)

Wollen's place was quite advanced, since its toilet did not require flushing.

My mother's memories of it aren't so fond as mine. It was 17 miles from the nearest paved road, telephone, or electricity, no easy place for a family—but there's a similar structure permanently enshrined in family lore.

It was discovered on a Sunday drive in the spring of 1960, near Raymond on the Peak-to-Peak highway. Necessity called for my mom, and so my father and my brothers and I desperately scanned the countryside from the car windows.

Soon we were rewarded—an outhouse down by the creek, no fence in the way. Mom raced down there, to discover a sign on the door: It Ain't Either. She pulled the door open, and it wasn't, either—it was a pump house.

And in the future, the few remaining privy structures will need that warning. It Ain't, Either. It's a tool shed or a photographer's prop or a perhaps even a designated historic landmark. But it won't answer the call of nature.

"Old-time Outhouse Is Going Way of all Flush" Copyright 1997 by Ed Quillen, reprinted with permission of the author. Originally published October 19, 1997, in the Sunday *Denver Post Empire Magazine*

Custer County Outhouses
BECKWITH RANCH OUTHOUSE

It is rare to find an outhouse in the process of restoration when most privies are being torn down. After years of neglect, the Beckwith Ranch, 5 miles north of Westcliffe along Colorado 69, was taken

The Beckwith Ranch north of Westcliffe. (Kenneth Jessen)

The outhouse behind the mansion at the Beckwith Ranch is being restored. (Kenneth Jessen)

over by the Friends of Beckwith Ranch. Using contributions and funds from the Colorado Historical Society, restoration work began in 2000, including the family outhouse.

The ranch was started in 1874 by brothers Elton and Edwin Beckwith. They built a ranching empire and a mansion to match. The ranch structures date to 1877.

Custer County Outhouses

BISHOP'S OUTHOUSE

Comfort station at Bishop Castle is primitive relative to the ornate castle. (Kenneth Jessen)

Located along the Greenhorn Highway (Colorado 165) southwest of Pueblo is possibly the most unique building in the American West. It is Bishop Castle, constructed by one man, Jim Bishop. It must be experienced to fully appreciate the size and complexity. Made from rubble stone and held together with concrete and steel, it is more of a work of art. One tower rises 160 feet above its surroundings. The castle has an external staircase extending up one of the flying buttresses to a large room. For those afraid of heights, there is an irregular spiral staircase in the interior. In keeping with his philosophy, Bishop asks nothing to see or enter the structure. He wants it open to rich and poor alike. However, there is a donation box and gift shop where souvenirs can be purchased.

He wrote a booklet called *Castle Building*, that he autographs "Jim Bishop (Castle Builder)." The booklet is less about castle building and more about fighting the bureaucracy of the U.S. Forest Service, the Colorado Department of Transportation, and most recently, Custer County officials.

In contrast to the ornate castle, there is a primitive-looking outhouse at the entrance to the grounds. It is made of lumber and sheets of plywood, has separate toilets for men and women, and is kept clean and functional. It is constructed over a concrete vault. On the side is written, "The future site of 250' high tower."

The dragon that extends from the front gable of Bishop Castle spews fire. (Kenneth Jessen)

Custer County Outhouses
WESTCLIFFE

This is one of two fully restored privies behind the historic Westcliffe schoolhouse. Hope Lutheran Church can be seen to the left. (Kenneth Jessen)

The Westcliffe schoolhouse was constructed in 1891 and has been fully restored, including its matching boys' and girls' outhouses. Westcliffe eclipsed the older and larger town of Silver Cliff, a little over a mile east. A land promotion scheme was headed by Dr. William A. Bell and several investors. They formed a town company with the knowledge that the Denver & Rio Grande would choose as its terminus their undeveloped piece of land. Bell was the vice president of the railroad.

Silver Cliff had grown quickly based on its nearby mines, and it was, for a time, Colorado's third-largest town. The creation of Westcliffe, with rail service, spelled the end to Silver Cliff's prosperity. When the railroad arrived in 1881, some of Silver Cliff's residents rolled their homes on logs to the new town.

Silver Cliff and Westcliffe combined their votes to take the county seat away from Rosita in 1886. A courthouse was constructed in Silver Cliff, but by 1928, much of the town had been abandoned. The county seat was then moved to Westcliffe.

Gunnison County Outhouses
ALPINE TUNNEL

At the west portal of the Alpine Tunnel was a small settlement of railroad workers who kept the Denver, South Park & Pacific narrow-gauge railroad open. At 11,500 feet, summers were short, and much of the work consisted of snow removal. At one time, there was a stone boardinghouse and stone engine house with an enclosed turntable. In 1906, fire destroyed all but the small depot. The following year, a new two-story frame boarding house was constructed and behind it, a two-stall outhouse.

This 1980 photograph shows the collapsed remains of the frame boarding house and its two-stall outhouse at the west portal of the Alpine Tunnel. (Ardie Schoeninger)

Work on the Alpine Tunnel began in 1880, and in 1882, trains were running through the tunnel to Gunnison. This 1,800-foot tunnel was the first drilled under the Continental Divide in North America. Operations were plagued by heavy snow at the approach to the tunnel and cave-ins within the tunnel. The tunnel was closed from 1890 to 1895 and was abandoned for good in 1910.

Today, the U.S. Forest Service has a display at the tunnel. The little depot has been restored and a short section of track, using the original rails, runs in front of the depot.

Gunnison County Outhouses
CRESTED BUTTE: TWO-STORY OUTHOUSES

Two-story outhouse behind what was once the Masonic Hall in Crested Butte. Benjamin Jessen is shown taking measurements for a scale drawing. (Kenneth Jessen)

Possibly the most famous outhouse in Colorado is the one behind the former Masonic Hall in Crested Butte. It is still functional and is a true two-story outhouse. Heavy winter snow with drifts in excess of 6 feet render the lower level inaccessible most of the winter. The upper level is joined to the main building by an elevated, covered walkway. There is an unused door, visible in the photograph, on the north side leading nowhere. Nail holes indicate that this second door once served another walkway originating from another building. The two levels are offset from each other so that the "business ends" are back to back thus allowing one pit to service both levels.

An extensive study of western evacuation was made by Norman Weis in his book, *The Two-Story Outhouse*. He traveled to four Canadian Provinces and eleven Western states during a 12-year period to study two-story outhouses. Weis related that at one time, there was a sign over the second-story entrance that read, "Anything over nine pounds must be lowered by rope." To attempt to comply with such a request, especially in urgent situations, seem ludicrous. The sign also required some interpretation, for example, nine pounds delivered all at once? How a rope could be deployed was also a mystery. The sign was probably placed there by some prankster.

Crested Butte was founded on coal mining, but it did have a smelter for precious metal ore. Howard E. Smith purchased most of the coal deposits in the area, and in 1879, he laid out the town naming it for nearby Crested Butte Mountain. In 1880, Crested Butte was incorporated, and the town continued to grow after the arrival of the narrow-gauge Denver & Rio Grande the following year. After the end of the coal-mining era, much of the town was abandoned. The ski industry revived the town, and few structures remain empty today.

Behind a yoga parlor and next to Mike and Beth Woodward's property is an abandoned two-story outhouse. Historic photographs of early Crested Butte show others. Crested Butte now has a sewage system and most of its outhouses are ornamental. There are still quite a few left standing and are best viewed by walking the town's alleys.

On the back wall of the historic Crested Butte city hall, constructed in 1883, is a flush mounted outhouse that once served both the first and second floors. As Crested Butte moved from a coal-mining economy into the ski resort-recreational era, the police office had to be expanded. An annex was constructed at the rear of the building.

Muriel Sibell Wolle, author of the classic ghost town book, *Stampede to Timberline*, took this photograph in 1944. The buildings this two-story outhouse served are long gone. (Denver Public Library)

This positioned part of the new office directly under the second level of the outhouse, and it had to be "decommissioned" to prevent police business from being interrupted.

This outhouse, in the backyard of Mike and Beth Woodward in Crested Butte, is strictly ornamental and has been moved away from its pit. (Kenneth Jessen)

Flush-mounted, two-story outhouse on the back of Crested Butte's city hall. (Kenneth Jessen)

Gunnison County Outhouses
CRYSTAL: KNOWN FOR ITS POWER PLANT

This old mining town is a little difficult to reach. It is located along a four-wheel drive road running between Marble and Crested Butte over Schofield Pass. The location is magnificent in a narrow valley surrounded by high mountains. Crystal was founded in 1880 based on the discovery of silver ore. The selection of the town site was restricted to the only flat area in the canyon. The town got a post office in 1882, but due to severe winter weather combined with its isolation, Crystal never grew beyond a few hundred individuals.

Crystal did have its share of stores and saloons, and it also had a newspaper and the Crystal Snowshoe Club. After the decline in the price of silver during the latter part of the nineteenth century, Crystal was slowly abandoned. By the beginning of the twentieth century, only one business remained, and in 1909, its post office closed. Its buildings stood empty for decades until the place was discovered as a summer paradise. Individuals began to purchase and restore the cabins for seasonal use.

Sheep Mountain Mill power plant below Crystal. (Kenneth Jessen)

Crystal is not known for its cabins or its outhouses. What makes Crystal famous is possibly the most photographed structure in all of Colorado. It is the power plant that once served the Sheep Mountain Mill just below the town site on the Crystal River.

Gunnison County Outhouses
IRIS

Iris outhouse photographed by Muriel Sibell Wolle. (Denver Public Library)

One of the most remote ghost towns in Colorado is located along the Gunnison-Saguache county line. The area consists of arid, rolling hills where gold was discovered in 1880. This led to the founding of several towns, including Iris.

Originally called Union Hill, the name was changed to Iris when a post office opened in 1894. The town never had more than about twenty structures including a couple of grocery stores. The low-grade ore never yielded much, and by the early part of the twentieth century, the deposits were either abandoned or exhausted. In 1903, Iris had but three residents, and soon after, the town was completely abandoned. When she was working on *Stampede to Timberline*, Muriel Sibell Wolle visited Iris in 1942 and photographed an outhouse near one of the abandoned mines. Today, the site is inaccessible to the public and is on private property.

Gunnison County Outhouses
MARBLE

Modern mountain property development abounds in the old town of Marble with new homes next to original structures. Most of the modern homes have indoor plumbing. However, there are still a few outhouses behind some of the older homes.

The town was founded based on vast marble deposits located in the Yule Creek drainage high above the town. The first quarry opened in 1884, and during succeeding years, a number of claims were filed. John B. Osgood, founder of Redstone and noted for his investments in coal, was one of the early investors. He had a block of marble quarried and sent to the 1893 Columbian Exposition for display. The following year, Yule marble was selected for Colorado's Capitol building.

Rail transportation was essential to the economical shipment of heavy marble blocks. In 1906, a railroad reached Marble, and in 1910, a 3.9-mile electric tramway was extended from Marble to the quarries.

Demand for marble eventually dropped, and the quarries closed in 1941. Marble was almost abandoned. After nearly 50 years, the quarries were reopened and continue to operate.

Part of a toilet bench is nailed to the side of an isolated outhouse in Marble. (Kenneth Jessen)

Gunnison County Outhouses
PITKIN: DEPOT PRIVY

The Denver, South Park & Pacific Pitkin depot has a matching outhouse. (Kenneth Jessen)

Farther up Quartz Creek from Ohio City is the town of Pitkin. It was originally called Quartzville, but some civic-minded soul changed the name in honor of Colorado Gov. Frederick W. Pitkin. A post office opened in 1879 coincident with the completion of a few permanent structures. The town continued its growth topping 1,000 people and nearly 200 structures. With arrival of the narrow-gauge Denver, South Park & Pacific in 1882, the town had a newspaper, bank, several hotels and many saloons. The town was dependent on silver mining, and as the price of silver fell during the late 1880s, Pitkin's population declined. Fire destroyed many of the buildings in 1898 and again in 1903. The town was never rebuilt, and after the abandonment of the railroad, Pitkin lost most of its residents.

Today, Pitkin is seasonally occupied. The old depot still stands, and although empty, it has been used as a home. It is painted blue and yellow and has a matching dual outhouse in back.

Gunnison County Outhouses

SANDY HOOK

A remarkable place for outhouses is Sandy Hook, located near the end of the graded road along Gold Creek, north of Ohio City. There are two log structures and one frame hotel. The buildings are seasonally occupied, and each has its own outhouse. There is a fourth outhouse in good condition by a large, stone foundation.

The outhouse behind the hotel is a dual "his" and "hers" type. It is two stories high and once had a plank walkway to the pair of doors. The hillside is virtually solid rock, and the lower portion forms the outhouse pit.

Remains of a plank walkway (right) can be seen leading to the doors of the dual "his" and "hers" outhouse that served the hotel (above) in Sandy Hook. (Kenneth Jessen)

Gunnison County Outhouses
TINCUP: MANY PRIVIES

A "CASHIER" sign identifies an outhouse located on the east edge of Tincup. (Kenneth Jessen)

Tincup has a one-to-one ratio between houses and privies. And, all of them appear to be in use now in this seasonally occupied mining town.

The town is located in the Taylor River drainage along Willow Creek. It was originally called Virginia City and was laid out in the large meadow where the three tributaries of Willow Creek converge. Aside from nearby mines, its economy was based on its location along a major supply route from the Taylor River Valley to the Chalk Creek drainage on the other side of Tincup Pass.

The town was founded in 1879 and soon had nearly 1,000 residents. During the first winter, however, nearly all departed for a warmer climate. The following spring, prospectors rushed back, and the population of Virginia City swelled to 1,500. Today, less than 100 call this place home, and most are seasonal residents.

Both Nevada and Montana had towns named Virginia City. Postal officials could see that this would lead to major mail delivery problems and insisted that the town change its name. The name selected was Tin Cup for the local mining district. In 1895, the name was changed to a single word, Tincup.

San Luis Valley Privies
BONANZA: EXTRA TALL OUTHOUSE

Bonanza is located in the northern part of the San Luis Valley, and its economy was based on silver mining. The Bonanza Mine was located in 1880, and the town was incorporated in November of that year. The largest mine was the Rawley. The town reached its peak in 1882 with an estimated population of 1,300. There were forty saloons and a house of ill repute high on a hill above the town. Not only did Bonanza have four hotels and many stores, but it also supported two newspapers. After the steady decline in silver prices during the late nineteenth century, most of the mines closed. There was a small boom in 1917, and Bonanza regained some of its population. In 1938, the town's population fell below the number required for continuation of its post office.

Today, only a few structures remain in this once sizable town. Almost all of the buildings in its business district are gone. Recently, the U.S. Forest Service removed the tailings from the Rawley Mine and Mill complex to try to restore water quality in Kerber Creek. Interpretive signs indicate the town's history, area roads and mine history.

This unusually tall, narrow outhouse sits in Bonanza behind an old foundation. (Kenneth Jessen)

San Luis Valley Privies
FORT GARLAND: RAILROAD OUTHOUSE

One of the outhouses in the town of Fort Garland is painted the same yellow color as buildings constructed by the Denver & Rio Grande. It is also the same type of construction and probably served the Fort Garland depot. (Kenneth Jessen)

Fort Garland was originally constructed as an army post in 1858. The flag was lowered for the last time in 1883, and Fort Garland passed through a number of property owners. It was eventually deeded to the Colorado Historical Society in 1945. Extensive restoration, however, was required to faithfully rebuild and reconstruct its buildings. Fort Garland is operated as a museum and is open to the public.

In 1878, the Denver & Rio Grande brought its narrow-gauge railroad through town, and Fort Garland became a shipping point for produce and cattle.

San Luis Valley Privies
GARCIA

Garcia is the oldest Spanish-speaking settlement in Colorado dating to 1849 when the Manzanares brothers brought their families into the region. They built La Plaza de los Manzanares on the northern outskirts of Costilla, and both communities fell within Colorado Territory. In 1869, the 37th parallel that defined the Colorado-New Mexico boundary line was officially surveyed and moved slightly north. This placed La Plaza de los Manzanares within Colorado and Costilla in New Mexico. The post office for La Plaza de los Manzanares opened in a store operated by the Garcia brothers, and in 1915, the post office and town took the name Garcia.

This outhouse in Garcia sits in a field west of the Catholic Church.

San Luis Valley Privies

JAROSO: KIRCHER'S OUTHOUSE OFFERS BEST TELEVISION RECEPTION

The Kircher's modern outhouse in Jaroso. It was Kircher's first project after moving from Lakewood. Note the TV antenna on the outhouse roof. (Kenneth Jessen)

Originally, the area around Jaroso was called *El Bosque de los Caballos* or wooded area where horses ranged. It became a town in 1910 with the arrival of the San Luis Southern and grew into a major trade center and a place where crops and livestock were brought from the surrounding area for shipment. The San Luis Southern had an interchange with the Denver & Rio Grande north at Blanca. The town fell upon hard times after the Great Depression, but today is being repopulated by artisans and others wishing to escape city life. Its post office remains open from 8 a.m. to noon weekdays.

A notable feature of Jaroso is the row of large trees down the center of its main street. This is unique for a small Colorado town.

Sculptor Lynn Kircher and his wife, Jane, are among those that rediscovered Jaroso. The only free television in this part of the San Luis Valley is when there is line of sight with San Antonio Mountain, located to the south of Jaroso. The best reception happens to be on the north side of Kircher's home on the roof of his outhouse.

San Luis Valley Privies

LOBATOS

These outhouses sit behind the Church of the Holy Family at Lobatos. (Kenneth Jessen)

The original name for Lobatos was Cenicero meaning "ashes." The name was used to describe the fine dust located southwest of the village, so fine that it flew up into the air like ashes from under the hoofs of draft animals passing along the trail. The original village of Cenicero was laid out during the mid-1850s as a plaza for protection against hostile Indians. When the twentieth century arrived, the plaza had a post office, S.P.M.D.T.U. hall and school. In 1902, the name of Cenicero was changed to Lobatos for the town's first postmaster. After World War II, many residents moved away to seek jobs in urban centers. Towns like Lobatos faded away.

Lobatos is located due east of Antonito, and what remains today is the Catholic Church, *La Iglesia de la Sagada Famila* or the Church of the Holy Family. The original building was constructed about 1877 and replaced by the present structure in 1952. The church, with its "Ladies" and "Men" outhouses in back, remains at the site, although the original plaza has long since crumbled away.

San Luis Valley Privies
LOS RINECONES MORADA

Penitente morada located near Los Rinecones. The building is no longer in use, and the cross has been removed. Its outhouse remains standing in the background. (Kenneth Jessen)

The Penitentes is a lay religious group that is tied to the beliefs of the Roman Catholic Church and practices in north-central New Mexico and Colorado's San Luis Valley. The full name is *Los Hermanos Penitentes* or The Penitent Brothers. Composed almost exclusively of men of Hispanic descent, they organized into local associations not only for religious reasons, but also for mutual aid. These fraternities preserved the Spanish language, customs and maintained a conservative faith in this isolated region. They constructed places of worship called *moradas*, and these buildings often co-existed with traditional Catholic churches in the small communities that dot this area. Today, it is difficult to determine what influence the Penitentes have on the region, but many of the moradas still survive.

San Luis Valley Privies
MESITA: MORMON CHURCH PRIVY

Mesita was one of several communities developed within the Sangre de Cristo Grant by the Costilla Estate Development Company around 1910. This town was originally called Hamburg and grew to several hundred people. Mormon settlers homesteaded in the area and constructed churches. After the San Luis Southern was officially abandoned in 1958, Mesita was left without rail service, and its population began to dwindle. The Church of the Latter Day Saints is now the dominant building in Mesita and is constructed of volcanic scoria found in the area.

The Church of the Latter Day Saints and its pristine outhouse dominate the remaining structures in Mesita. (Kenneth Jessen)

San Luis Valley Privies
SAN FRANCISCO

Abandoned, this outhouse in San Francisco sits by a parking lot next to what might have been a farmers' market. Note the broken skylight. (Kenneth Jessen)

A land grant was given to settlers by the Mexican government in 1842 within what is now the Colorado portion of the San Luis Valley. It was called the Conejos Grant, and settlers were required to cultivate the land and never leave. Failure to comply meant forfeiture. The towns were to be well fortified. The earliest attempts at settlement met with failure at the hands of hostile Ute Indians. The first attempt at settling San Francisco was in 1843, followed by a second attempt in 1846. In 1854, San Francisco finally took hold and has been occupied continuously ever since. The first school district was formed in 1858.

San Luis Valley Privies
SUMMITVILLE

The first gold discovery at the foot of South Mountain west of Del Norte was made in 1870. Summitville was soon established near Wightman Creek at an elevation of 11,200 feet. At first, the town was seasonally occupied until permanent structures were built that allowed miners to survive the harsh winters. The population fluctuated between 300 and 600 until new discoveries were made. With the advent of large-scale mining during the 1930s, as many as 1,500 lived in Summitville. Mining continued using new heap leaching technology into the 1990s. A serious spill of toxic potassium cyanide into the Alamosa River ended all mining operations at Summitville.

This Summitville outhouse was photographed in 1975. (Ardie Schoeninger)

San Luis Valley Privies
VIEJO SAN ACACIO

In the southern part of the San Luis Valley, Viejo (old) San Acacio was founded as Plaza Abajo or Lower Culebra. It was settled in 1853 and has the oldest standing church in Colorado, constructed in 1856. The church has been completely restored and is in excellent condition. Oral tradition holds that settlers came into this area during the 1840s, but that a permanent town was not established until years later. The miraculous appearance of San Acacio on horseback occurred during a raid by Ute Indians on the early Spanish-speaking settlers. This vision frightened away the Indians, and the town's people were spared. It was at this point that the name of the town became San Acacio.

With the arrival of the San Luis Southern, a new town named San Acacio was formed a short distance away, and the original town became Viejo (old) San Acacio. Viejo San Acacio and its remarkable church are located about a half mile south of Colorado 142 and about 2 miles east of "new" San Acacio.

Viejo (old) San Acacio has the oldest standing church in Colorado, constructed in 1856 and fully restored. The outhouse serving the Viejo San Acacio Catholic Church is kept spotless, a tribute to the local parish. (Kenneth Jessen)

chapter 6

OUTHOUSES OF

WESTERN COLORADO

ALTA

A night trip for the miners to the outhouse behind the Alta boardinghouse was a chilling experience. Alta, located in San Miguel County, was founded around a rich lode of gold ore discovered in 1878.

The Alta mine and mill complex operated through World War II. Fire destroyed the mill and surface buildings near the mine in 1948. The ore reserves were insufficient to reopen the mine.

The Alta boardinghouse privy looks cold after an autumn snowfall. (Kenneth Jessen)

The boardinghouse, its outhouse and a few of the homes were spared by the devastating 1948 fire. (Kenneth Jessen)

BEDROCK

Copper ore was discovered in 1898 along the Dolores River south of Paradox Valley. The dominant mine was the Cashin, and the resulting mining boom led to the founding of Bedrock. The town acted as a supply point and an amusement center for the miners. Soon the town had two hotels and two saloons. There was also a doctor's office. Bedrock's post office opened in 1883 and closed in 1903. It reopened in 1911, and the post office at the Cashin Mine eventually was moved to Bedrock.

In *Colorado Travelore*, published in 1938, the author noted that Bedrock was so tough that the miners kept mountain lions as house cats. The author also told of a U.S. Geological Survey team driven off by masked men in 1910.

The only occupied structure in Bedrock today is its historic store. It was constructed about 1876 and has been used almost continuously since it opened. The store was added to the Colorado State Register of Historic Properties in 1993.

The outhouse at the Bedrock store has a crescent moon ventilator over the door. A piece of the seat is missing making it somewhat uncomfortable for making a deposit in a sitting position. (Kenneth Jessen)

CAPITOL CITY: LEE MANSION PRIVY

Muriel Sibell Wolle photographed the Lee Mansion and its outhouse at Capitol City in 1949. The mansion had been abandoned for many years and was slowly crumbling away as evidenced by the hole in the brick wall. (Denver Public Library)

Capitol City, originally called Galena City, was established in the spring of 1877 in a beautiful meadow west of Lake City at the confluence of the north and south forks of Henson Creek. Despite its remote location, its founders believed it could become the capital of Colorado. George S. Lee was especially optimistic about the town's location and constructed a remarkable, two-story brick mansion at the site in 1879. It looked out of place among the primitive log cabins common to the area. Lee hoped his mansion would at least become the summer home for Colorado's governor.

Capitol City never grew beyond a mining camp and did not even become the Hinsdale County seat. Its decline began as the price of silver dropped during the late nineteenth century. Lee abandoned his mansion, and it slowly crumbled away. Nothing remains today. The author of *Stampede to Timberline*, Muriel Sibell Wolle, photographed the Lee Mansion in 1949 for her classic ghost town book.

CORTEZ

County health departments throughout Colorado have banned outhouses over unlined pits. To satisfy county inspectors, such as those in Montezuma County, one practice is to move the outhouse away from its pit and tip it over.

This outhouse was tipped over possibly to demonstrate that it is no longer "active." It is visible from Colorado 160 south of Cortez. (Kenneth Jessen)

DOVE CREEK

How Dove Creek became the Dolores County seat is a strange story beginning with the mining boom in Rico. Isolated by poor roads and high mountain passes, Rico established its own mining district apart from other districts in the San Juan Mountains. To reach the county seat in Ouray required several days, and during winter, the trip became impossible most of the time. The Colorado Legislature solved this problem in 1881 by creating Dolores County from the western half of Ouray County and naming Rico the new county seat.

Rico gradually declined as the economic center of Dolores County when its mineral resources were depleted. In the meantime, the western half of the county became a rich agricultural area. The town of Dove Creek was established in 1912, and by 1940, it dominated the region. A movement began to move the county seat to Dove Creek, and in 1941, the required two-thirds vote was met.

Mike Barrett was raised on the east side of Dove Creek. Around 1930, Barrett's father constructed an oversize outhouse with two holes and a double hip roof. So large was its interior that Barrett's aunt once quipped, "Put a stove in it, and I'll rent it from you!" During the 1990s, Barrett's nephew added a copper cupola.

This oversize outhouse, at the east end of Dove Creek, was constructed around 1930. (Kenneth Jessen)

DUNTON

Dunton is an isolated mining town located on the West Dolores River 10.2 miles over a graded dirt road from U.S. 550. Established in 1885, it was supported by several small mines. After the construction of a stamp mill, it may have reached a peak population of 300. Its post office opened in 1892 and remained open until 1954, well after the mines closed.

Years after the abandonment of Dunton, the site was purchased as a combination cattle and dude ranch. Hunting, fishing and the hot springs are its main attractions.

Outhouse with sloping walls at Dunton. (Ardie Schoeninger)

GATEWAY

Sitting over a concrete vault, this Gateway outhouse is located along Colorado 141. (Kenneth Jessen)

Gateway is located at the confluence of West Creek and the Dolores River along an old Ute trail. The name was suggested by the prominent break in the rimrock along the Dolores River. Gateway is at the south end of Unaweep Canyon, a geological oddity. Water flows out of both ends of the valley as West and East creeks. Gateway got its post office in 1903 and school in 1914. Electricity was not available in Gateway until 1952, and Colorado 141 was not paved until 1958.

The McCarty gang had a cabin in nearby Sinbad Valley during the 1890s. Sew-'Em-Up Mesa got its name from the rustlers that sewed up the old brands and re-branded stolen cattle.

LAKE CITY

Historian Grant Houston pointed out a fabulous stone outhouse located in an alley by a small, stone cottage. The builder of the two structures had just finished this project in 1952 and then suddenly passed away. Nearby is another unique privy painted blue with a yellow crescent. The Hinsdale County Museum has a men's and women's dual privy that once sat by the Denver & Rio Grande depot. It was constructed in 1889 when the railroad arrived in Lake City. In 1990, the Hinsdale Historical Society distinguished itself by publishing the first Colorado county-specific outhouse calendar.

Prospectors came into the Lake City area as early as 1869. Promising ore was discovered in 1872 southwest of Lake San Cristobal. No claims could be made since it was within Ute territory. The following year, the Brunot Agreement was signed where the Ute Indians gave up all of their ancestral land in the San Juan Mountains. This opened the door for the establishment of a permanent town.

Both gold and silver ore was discovered by toll road builder Enos Hotchkiss. After removing what he believed was all of the ore from his Golden Fleece Mine, he and his partners

The man who constructed this beautiful stone privy passed away soon after he completed the job. (Kenneth Jessen)

Another privy gem in Lake City is this blue outhouse with a yellow crescent painted on its door. (Kenneth Jessen)

abandoned the claim. It later yielded $250,000 under new ownership.

The Golden Fleece brought in a flood of prospectors. In 1875, the Lake City Town Company was formed to sell lots. Although San Juan City in Antelope Park was the first county seat, Lake City took the title by popular vote the same year.

Colorado's most notorious cannibal, Alfred Packer, dined on his victims near Lake City during the winter of 1873-1874. His sensational trial took place in the Hinsdale County courthouse in Lake City. Packer was found guilty and was the first person sentenced to death in Hinsdale County. He was also the first Coloradan convicted of murder by cannibalism.

RED MOUNTAIN PASS

Red Mountain Pass is located along U.S. 550 between Silverton and Ouray and was one of the most active mining areas in Colorado. The mines supported a number of settlements, including Sheridan Junction on Red Mountain Pass. The first rich chimney of silver-galena ore was discovered at the Yankee Girl in 1882 and heralded the beginning of a mining boom.

Due to the limitation of ore wagons and mule trains, only the richest ore could be economically mined and shipped to smelters in Silverton and Ouray. Lower-grade ore was discarded. With the arrival of the narrow-gauge Silverton Railroad in 1888, built from Silverton over Red Mountain Pass, lower-grade ore then became profitable to mine. Mining activity tapered off toward the end of the nineteenth century with silver prices falling below half of their former value. Using tunnels for both transportation and drainage, mining continued on a limited basis through the 1930s. Today, fires and heavy winter snows have taken their toll, and only a small fraction of the original structures remain.

Mine outhouse sitting on cribbing near Red Mountain Pass. (Cyndi Trombly)

SILVERTON: MOYLE BROTHERS BAND

This photograph of the Moyle Brothers Band, seen standing on the front porch, was taken around 1886. The small boy by the base drum is Alfred Moyle, son of Mathew. Note that the Moyle family outhouse is at the end of their front porch. (Denver Public Library)

An outhouse in plain view is quite rare, but in this case, there may have been practical reasons for its location. The Moyle family outhouse was at the end of their front porch and given the prodigious amount of snow, eliminated the need to keep a path shoveled to the structure. The location was more convenient for children. The steep hillside behind the home limited outhouse location. Their source of fresh water was likely a spring or creek behind the home. To avoid contamination, the privy must be lower than the water supply.

The Moyle Brothers Band was famous throughout the San Juan Mountains. The core of the band consisted of brothers James, Mathew and William, with other family members participating. The Moyle home was on Sultan Mountain south of Silverton near the mine worked by the brothers.

chapter 7

COMPOSTING
COMFORT STATIONS

GRIZZLY CREEK

Designed by Phillip E. Flores and constructed for the Colorado Department of Transportation, the Grizzly Creek composting comfort station has no impact on the surrounding soil or water. It is ecologically friendly. (Kenneth Jessen)

The Grizzly Creek comfort station represents the evolution of the simple, unlined pit-style outhouse of yesteryear to an ecologically sensitive toilet.

Prior to the construction of I-70 through Glenwood Canyon, there was a small picnic area and a gas station where Grizzly Creek enters the Colorado River. The problem faced by landscape architect Phillip E. Flores was to preserve and enhance the natural features of this area.

Drilling into the soil structure determined it would not be possible to construct a comfort station with a vaulted toilet that would require pumping. The porous alluvial fan from Grizzly Creek combined with the proximity of the comfort station site to the Colorado River produced a high water table. A sewage line to Glenwood Springs also was not practical due to the terrain and distance. This limited the choices to a composting toilet, and the Clivius-Multrum system was selected.

Composting takes place below each toilet in a large container. Material containing bacteria that looks like sawdust is added. This starts the composting process. Once the container is full of decomposed sewage, it is moved across the lower level of the comfort station to an elevator where it is raised to the roof. Here it is loaded on a truck and hauled to a disposal facility.

The waste products from men and women differ. This requires switching sides periodically, and to accomplish this, sliding placards are used in the lobby, one labeled "Men" and the other labeled "Women." The design of the comfort station is such that the urinals are in a separate room. Doors on either side can be opened or closed according to usage.

The "Women" and "Men" signs in the lobby of the Grizzly Creek comfort station slide past each other and are switched periodically to balance the waste products. (Kenneth Jessen)

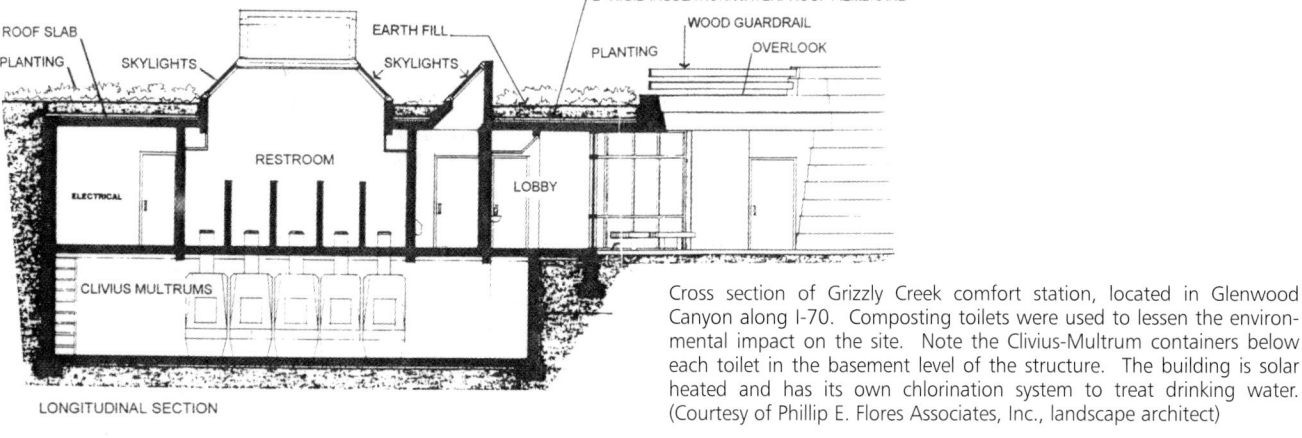

Cross section of Grizzly Creek comfort station, located in Glenwood Canyon along I-70. Composting toilets were used to lessen the environmental impact on the site. Note the Clivius-Multrum containers below each toilet in the basement level of the structure. The building is solar heated and has its own chlorination system to treat drinking water. (Courtesy of Phillip E. Flores Associates, Inc., landscape architect)

COLORADO'S WORLD-CLASS OUTHOUSE
by Thomas Noel

WORLD-CLASS status may come with the new airport or baseball team. Meanwhile, Coloradans can console themselves in a new comfort station. It is on I-70 in Glenwood Canyon at the Grizzly Creek Rest Area.

This world-class 10-holer dwarfs the famed two-story outhouse rising above Crested Butte's blizzards. Cherry Creek Shopping Center's marble-walled bathrooms cannot compete on either landscaping or ecological grounds. Grizzly Creek even outshines Georgetown's Victorian water closet. That lily-white six-holer behind the Hamill House Museum has three walnut seats in front reserved for the Hamill family, while backside plain pine holes accommodated their servants. The domestics used their half of the privy, according to excavating archaeologists, to hide empty liquor bottles and broken Haviland china.

"Instead of the usual pit stop," supervising landscape architect Phillip E. Flores noted, "our design team tried to provide an inspirational respite. We rejuvenated Grizzly Creek with pools, riffles, waterfalls and an island. More than 40,000 native plants have been installed at the site, which used to be a gas station, orchard, fruit stand and mobile home park. The new concrete, glass and tile facility is solar and earth-sheltered. This rest stop is not just for motorists. There's an equestrian staging area, hike-bike trail access and raft-kayak launch."

"To protect the watershed, we used self-composting, waterless, Clivius-Multrum toilets," explained Flores, a veteran Denver landscape architect whose next project is planning a better Mousetrap for I-70 and I-25. "Grizzly can hold two years worth of deposits before removal and recycling as compost. Men and women," Flores elaborated, "deposit different amounts with different chemical composition. So we have to switch restrooms regularly for better organic harmony. That's why we have the tamper-proof, switchable sex sign in the front lobby."

After arriving at Grizzly Creek on four wheels, two wheels, water, horseback or on foot, there is more than one thing to do. Taking a hike, for instance. While the nearby Hanging Lake Trail usually seems jammed, Grizzly Creek Trail is a little used, gentle forest hike. It follows the ruins of an antique wooden flume up Grizzly Creek, which out roars even I-70.

Colorado Department of Transportation engineers and affiliated architects and contractors rose to the challenge. Their beautiful, double ribbon of highway is tinted to match the craggy canyon walls. I-70 flows through the canyon, sometimes rimming the river, sometimes double-decking, sometimes floating over the treetops. Cantilevered lanes, 39 bridges, tunnels and a hike-bike path generally complement the work of the Colorado River. To heal construction scars, an army of workers sculpted and stained newly exposed rock to match the patina of the unmolested canyon walls. Over 100,000 hardy native trees and shrubs have been planted to compensate for what has been lost. And Grizzly Creek received Colorado's finest comfort station.

The station resembles a Mayan temple. Its stepped walls, terraces and rock gardens echo the sandstone, limestone and granite strata of the surrounding canyon. The vented skylight on top is the centerpiece of a rooftop deck plaza. There you can survey the river, creek, highway and Union Pacific railroad tracks. Here, too, you may catch a few whiffs. As the cleaning lady put it, "Yeah, it's a swell place, but it's still an outhouse!"

Published in the *Denver Post*, July 11, 1991. Reprinted by permission of the author.

MAROON CREEK

One of Colorado's most scenic areas is at the head of Maroon Creek. The road begins outside Aspen and ends in 11 miles at the foot of Pyramid Peak, 14,018 feet with North Maroon Peak and Maroon Peak, also over 14,000 feet, just a little over 2 miles away. The parking lot is near the edge of Maroon Lake with a trail leading to Crater Lake and beyond. The dilemma faced by the U.S. Forest Service is the large number of visitors into the area, some years totals reached a quarter of a million. Not wishing to increase the parking lot size, visitors use a bus service from Memorial Day until autumn.

To provide adequate toilet facilities, a Bio-Sun composting system was selected. Self-contained and solar powered, it is truly environmentally friendly in this sensitive area. Air is injected continuously into the composting chamber to create an aerobic environment thus eliminating any odor. Unlike a septic system, the Bio-Sun unit has microorganisms that use oxygen to decompose the waste material producing carbon dioxide and water vapor.

Because the site selected is in the direct path of winter avalanches, the vents extend into the woods. The air intakes are carefully hidden in

This entrance to the Maroon Creek comfort station faces southwest toward the mountains. (Kenneth Jessen)

the artificial rock facade. The entire Maroon Creek facility is buried under a mound of rock and dirt that has been carefully landscaped to blend into its surroundings.

The Bio-Sun system is waterless and does not require periodic pumping of waste material. Once finished compost is achieved, a small amount of humus is all that remains. Unlike the Clivius-Multrum system, a single composting chamber does not require that the men's and women's sides to be periodically reversed.

The main entrance to the Maroon Creek comfort station faces the parking lot. The backdrop is composed of the Maroon Bells, among the most rugged mountains within Colorado. This photograph was taken prior to landscaping. (Courtesy Bio-Sun Systems)

Despite every effort by the U.S. Forest Service to provide a comfort station that blends in, this unique structure has its critics. Joanne Ditmer of the *Denver Post* wrote, "Maroon Bells, the awesome rock formation with a lovely mountain lake in the foreground, has been blocked from arriving view by a humongous pile of rocks and dirt that's supposed to make a 10-stall restroom under it blend into the landscape." The *Rocky Mountain News* referred to the architecture as "Flintstone-esque," and the *Denver Post* called it the Taj Mahal of outhouses. Some of those in Aspen were offended by the aesthetics of the building, but a lot of the criticism centered on its cost and the fee charged to enter the area. All of these objections will probably melt away with time as the extensive landscaping matures and all but the entrances disappear from view.

The interior of the Maroon Creek comfort station is clean and inviting, unlike U.S. Forest Service privies of the past. (Courtesy Bio-Sun Systems)

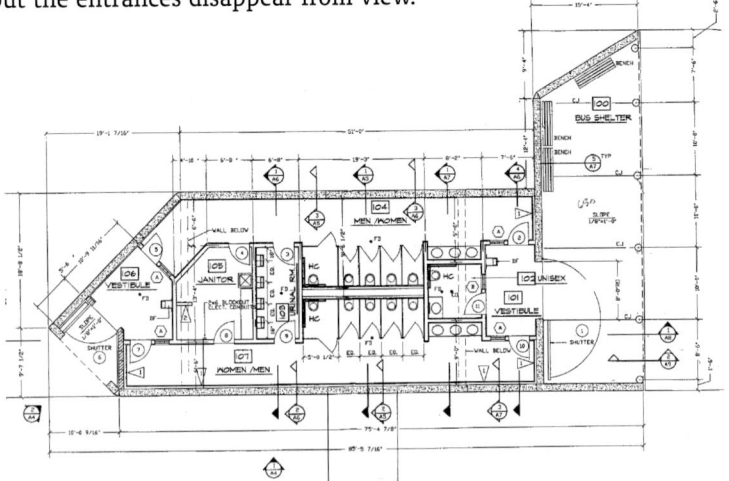

Although this floor plan shows the men's and women's sides as being interchangeable, unlike the Clivius-Multrum system, switching sides is not necessary for the Bio-Sun composting system. Except for its entrances, the entire structure is buried under a mound of dirt and rock as protection from avalanches. (Courtesy of the U.S. Forest Service)

Appendix A: Great Plains Privies

by Charles O. Collins, Department of Geography, University of Northern Colorado

Centrally located WPA Sanitary Privy sits among the abandoned farm buildings in northeastern Colorado. (Kenneth Jessen)

A case could be made for studying the privy as an act of culture conservation. The little houses are rapidly disappearing from the Great Plains and elsewhere. They fall victim to modernization, Halloween pranksters, and high-school seniors searching for homecoming bonfire fuel. Irate farmers truck the little, white houses to town to protest farm policies emanating from their larger namesake. In fact, during the course of this study, a discouraging number of privies disappeared, and apart from photographs and notes, culture clues were lost. But there is another reason to study the privy.

Mainstream American taboos concerning bodily functions, notably elimination and contact with human wastes, dictate all manner of circumspection. As one consequence, the privy has been virtually invisible to many prominent America-watchers. Thoreau, de Voto and even the irreverent Twain studiously avoided the topic. While some contemporary writers acknowledge the little house, it is typically to indulge in nostalgia or bawdy prose, with little analysis or social interpretation. Thus avoidance, or disguising humor, characterizes social traits that make us uncomfortable, but which are critical in understanding our culture: competitiveness, attitudes about death and defilement are but a few examples. Likewise, a privy study represents this same category of avoided topics. At stake is a better understanding of past attitudes and social values that have direct links to contemporary cultural behavior.

METHOD USED IN THIS STUDY

Rural landscape topics are products of habitually reading the roadside. The view may offer haystackers and dugouts, silos and corncribs; eventually, however, a unique element or pattern beckons the eye. Such an approach

A homemade single-seater outhouse sits on the Groseclose property located 35 miles northeast of Wray in Yuma County. (Mary Jane Groves)

suggested that private outdoor privies, typically associated with a bygone era, survive in surprising numbers in the farmyards of the Great Plains. From the most modest, homemade single-seaters to the proverbial brick model, from two-story affairs to federally funded family models, hundreds of artifact privies were located, measured, plotted and photographed.

Once the privy became the focus of attention, observations were recorded by site-situation categories. For example, how near or distant was the privy to the dwelling, to other buildings and to the nearest public road? What was the privy's orientation relative to prevailing wind, to the house, other buildings and the nearest road? How was the privy associated with other structures in the farmyard? On which side of the house was it placed? Was the privy site open and visible, isolated or secluded? After several hundred observations, various patterns emerged and preliminary hypotheses were possible.

To test the initial survey observations an intensive sample was taken along a continuous 30-mile segment of state highway in eastern Colorado. This transect spanned portions of two counties and ran through irrigated farmland, yielding 105 farmsteads fronting directly onto the highway.

Each of the 105 farmsteads was studied and field notes indexed the following information: (1) presence or absence of privy structure; (2) type and condition of structure; (3) relative location; (4) orientation; and (5) relative visibility of structure from the nearest public access point. The sample produced fifty-two standing privies.

A second non-random sample was taken to determine the distance separating privies from dwellings. Twenty-five examples were selected based on proximity to the author's home. This sample also was used to study the relative visibility of the privy from the dwelling. Four observations were duplications from the larger sample of 105 farmsteads.

The combined samples revealed only minor variations from the general Great Plains survey in terms of privy construction, type, orientation and placement. Evident in both the survey and the samples was a set of culturally dictated strategies to integrate the privy into the farmscape. Integration in this context, however, was not for the typical reasons of embellishment, efficiency or overall landscape design as is typical for other elements of the farmyard. Rather, integration of the privy in the common landscape was predicated on a "geography" of avoidance and disguise.

PRIVY HISTORY

A history of the privy in the Great Plains can be divided into three stages. Such amenities were rare during the pioneer era, as there was neither much material nor motivation for their construction. Heyday for the little houses arrived during the late nineteenth and early twentieth centuries when official concern about rural health and sanitation legislated construction of thousands of "sanitary facilities." Today, privies are a relict feature on the Great Plains, although a surprisingly tenacious one.

From a conceptual perspective, it is important to recognize that throughout their history, privies changed very little in size, style or placement. This is a radical departure when compared to other elements of the common landscape. In contrast to the evolutionary enlargement and embellishment of houses or churches, the changeless nature of the privy suggests deep-seated social values and constraints, and further recommends the little house as a significant cultural symbol.

No matter where they are located, privies have changed little over the years in size, style or placement. This particular unit is located along Fourmile Canyon Road by a mine in Boulder County. (Kenneth Jessen)

This "six pack" privy is located at the Chaparral RV park near the Spinney Mountain Reservoir in South Park. There are three separate toilets on the womens' side and three on the mens' side. (Kenneth Jessen)

Many Great Plains settlers managed without a privy, counting on isolation for privacy and the natural environment to provide sanitation. Traditionally, people sought a secluded area where they tried to prevent odors by carefully selecting a different place each time. The folk association of odors with disease discouraged accumulation of wastes in a privy, or any location near the dwelling and promoted the scattering of human wastes where the "well known" cleansing properties of soil, sunlight and rain (not to mention scavenging hogs) provided "natural" waste disposal.

Public health campaigns to promote sanitary privies had to contend with this habit of "promiscuous defecation."

It should not be necessary to point out that such attitudes were more convenient in the eastern and southern states than on the Great Plains. However, pioneers brought their habits with them, and consequently turned to the wheat field, shelterbelt, pigpen or corral as an acceptable "privy."

In cases where modesty was demanded, purchased lumber provided a privy, although the family budget might dictate that they continue to live in a sod house and perhaps worship in a sod church. Why "prairie marble" was not more frequently used for privy building is a matter of conjecture. Surely, such a facility would have been dark, dank, and poorly ventilated. Moreover, the weight of sod walls perched on the lip of a privy pit was an inherently precarious arrangement. But above all was the matter of maintenance: a sod privy could not be moved but had to be mucked out. A wood structure was portable and could easily be moved from site to site as need arose.

The second privy era spanned the late decades of the nineteenth century and the early years of the twentieth century. Increasing population and a more enlightened attitude toward personal and community health promoted farm and village privies. Still, state or federal legislation was often necessary to assure that every Great Plains resident had access to a privy. Apathy sprang from ignorance, but there were those who opposed privies on philosophical grounds. Some males asserted that privies were strictly for women and children, and for an adult male to use them was unmanly. In a similar vein, a

Cribbing is used to contain the waste products in this modern privy in Summit County. Rocky conditions prevent digging a pit. (Ardie Schoeninger)

few "rural authorities" insisted that privies or water closets never be allowed inside houses as this was a sign of effeminacy. Yet in most communities, common sense, or the health authorities, prevailed and nearly every residence was served by a privy.

Despite nearly ubiquitous indoor plumbing, the privy persists on the Great Plains today in surprising, if dwindling numbers. The transect suggests that almost one-half of the farmsteads still have a standing privy. However, this survival rate should not be projected to the entire Great Plains owing to the comparatively late date of settlement in the sampled area. Of the privies that remain, some are preserved for nostalgia sake. A few are associated with migrant housing. But the greatest number survive as a "backup system," as a convenience to those working outside, or as one respondent pointed out, for "times when a lot of company comes over."

DEVELOPMENT OF THE LITTLE HOUSE

Although it is possible to chart the growing acceptance of the privy, never was there a consensus on what constituted adequate human waste disposal. Government and private views were usually at odds, the former consistently opting for more sanitary, and thus, more elaborate strategies. But given the conservative nature of most Great Plains farmers, it is not surprising that they usually chose the least bothersome response.

Incontestably, the privy has been the least elaborate and most unchanging element of the built landscape on the Great Plains. Whether an attribute of the hard-pressed, tight-fisted or merely traditional nature of local residents, it remains that an elaborate privy did not fit in the scheme of things. A family might announce its economic and social station by its house, or more commonly the barn, but not by size or style of outhouse. And while a larger chicken coop or a better barn might multiply the farmer's investment, the privy promised no such profits. So for motives of frugality, modesty and tradition, the Great Plains privy was not a grand structure. In point of fact, 92 percent, of the sampled privies were the single-seat variety and all were of wood. Even the occasional multi-seat "family model" was strictly functional and without embellishments.

Most home privies measured no more than 4 feet on a side and 7 to 8 feet at the roof peak. Wood was the material of choice, either wide boards fixed vertically to a balloon frame of 2 by 4's or milled siding lapped horizontally in a manner identical to the house and barn. Most privies were small enough to be built of scrap lumber left from the house or barn, a fact that helped the little structure blend into the landscape. Simplicity was the hallmark of the home-built privy: single slope or shed roofs were favored for ease of construction (and fewer corners for wasp nests), and the door was just enough boards fastened together to cover the entry. Windows, ventilators, seat-lids, decorative trim or "moons" were uncommon. Painted privies most commonly received a coat of white (80 percent of sample), the symbol of purity—and a navigational aid to nighttime visitors.

But, not all privies were of wood. Alternative building materials included tar or "brick" paper, poles

A stone privy, such as this one on Squaw Mountain, is relatively rare. A clean-out door is situated on the lower part of the structure. Most outhouses are constructed of lighter material so that they can be lifted or slid over a new pit. (Kenneth Jessen)

covered with burlap, canvas or feed sacks, baled hay, sheet metal, and once in a great while, the proverbial brick model. Stable and Halloween-proof such a structure might be, but its great shortcoming was maintenance: the only reasonable route for cleaning the pit was through the seat hole. Several sheet metal outhouses also were discovered, but they, too, were rare. One can only imagine the frigidness of these little tin boxes in January, their stifling closeness in July and the damage to anyone's hearing unfortunate enough to be caught inside during a Great Plains' hailstorm.

The typical privy contained one or two seats. A few larger family models had graduated seat sizes, with the littlest often tucked protectively between the adult ports. Occasionally seats were built at different levels to accommodate various sized users, or more simply, a footrest was added for the short-legged. But given to prevailing etiquette and modesty—mothers were known to remove corset ads from catalogs left in the privy lest young boys become obsessed with sex—it is difficult to imagine much joint occupancy. In light of such attitudes, multiple-seat privies were correspondingly rare, i.e., only four of the fifty-two transect sample examples had more than one seat. Even these structures were only slightly larger than the standard one-holer.

GOVERNMENT INVOLVEMENT IN THE PRIVY

As public health agencies were empowered to improve rural sanitation, watertight or chemical closet privies were initially proposed as the only safe means of human waste disposal. Public acceptance of such contraptions was virtually nil, however, since they were considered too expensive, too complicated and too troublesome to maintain. In the face of resistance, at least a few health officials admitted that chemical and watertight designs subjected the user to "more or less splashing" and could not tolerate newspaper or corn cobs. A few sanitarians in a compromising mood acknowledged that to be accepted and widely used privies had to provide for "reduction of the personal element involved in maintenance." In everyday language, this meant no manual cleaning lest there be physical contact with privy contents.

The public's message eventually reached official ears. Washington hastened to explain that minimizing cost always had been a "virtue in the conduct of privy sanitation" and followed the announcement with a flurry of free, officially recommended privy plans "within the purse limits of the poor" and the carpentry skills of "any 14-year-old school boy of average intelligence." Predictably, these were modest in size and simple in design. However, home-styled privies and the attitudes behind them were even more rudimentary.

Health agencies capitulated on several points. Promotion of chemical and other closed systems languished or was tempered as health agencies and citizens jointly assessed a practical three-fold option: (1) no privy, (2) an elaborate but unpopular sanitary privy and (3) a simple but acceptable privy. What prevailed in most rural areas was a little house placed over a pit. Though it provided less than ideal sanitation, the arrangement was inexpensive, and because it was portable, required virtually no maintenance. For the citizenry, and some health professionals, the crowning virtue of the pit privy was the public's willingness to use it.

Located west of Greeley, this WPA Sanitary Privy, is the relatively rare, multi-seat family model. Most of these units are of the single-seat variety. (Charles Collins)

THE WPA SANITARY PRIVY

The embodiment of public-private compromise on rural sanitation was the Works Progress Administration privy of the 1930s. Its design incorporated features that promoted sanitation, including concrete floors and pit, ventilator, screening, "automatic" seat lid, self-closing door and generally tight construction. Still, homeowner attitudes were served concerning small size, portability and low cost. Acceptance of this compromise is reflected in the transect sample where 27 percent of the privies were WPA built and all were single-seaters instead of the multiple seat family models. Both models were available to homeowners for the cost of materials (about $35 for one-holers) with labor provided "free" by the WPA, or as it came to be popularly known, the "Relief Administration" or "We Piddle Around."

Given the government's penchant to largeness, the small size of federally subsidized privies was a victory for modesty. Not only were the little houses unobtrusive and easily screened from view, but they were reasonably movable despite the concrete floor and riser.

The pit beneath a movable privy did not have to be cleaned, rather, when it neared capacity or became embarrassingly redolent, the little house was shifted to a new site and the old pit buried. Clearly, however, this was not the intent of the WPA design. Officially, the privy house was to be moved aside while the concrete pit was scooped out and then the structure replaced. In this way, sanitation and cleaning were facilitated, though at the cost of direct physical contact with the privy's contents. But the obvious solution to many a farmer was to move the privy to a new earth pit instead of replacing it on the original site. Not only did this reduce the frequency of an unappealing chore, it meant that no one had to get down in the privy pit to "muck" it out. In the moving process, of course, the sanitary effectiveness of the privy was compromised, but not to the degree once believed. Percolation or seepage of privy contents in most soils was restricted to the immediate area of the privy, perhaps no more than a foot beyond the pit.

So standard was the practice of moving privies that some builders fitted a metal lifting ring into the roof that allowed the structure to be conveniently moved. The new pit was normally dug nearby, in part, because this provided dirt to cover the old one. Also, it made life a bit less confusing to the young and the very old who were accustomed to a particular location. A privy might remain at the same site for a year or more since conventional wisdom found it better to have a small privy over a deep pit than a large one over a shallow hole. But in the final analysis, the new site was near the old because only certain locations in the yard were culturally suitable for a privy. Though the building was small and portable, and farmyards were large, proper privy placement was not a random act but a decision requiring experience and sensitivity to prevailing cultural and social values.

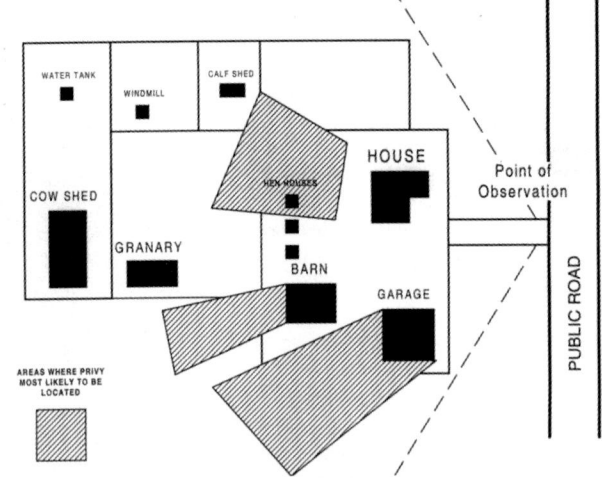

Farmyard plan with privy out of sight. (Based on a drawing by Charles Collins)

PRIVY LOCATION, A REFLECTION OF AMERICAN CULTURE

At this juncture, it becomes critical to more closely focus on the spatial context within which the privy should be analyzed. Traditionally, farmyards have been large and filled with a variety of structures and spaces devoted to specific functions.

Anglo-American culture tends to organize, label, and use its living spaces, including the distinction between the "aggressively public" front yard and the more private areas behind the house. Predictably then, no privy pattern on the Great Plains is so consistent as this: the privy "belongs" behind the house. Perhaps in other regions and other cultures this is less axiomatic. Prevailing thinking expressed the opinion that outhouses were necessary of course, and should be provided, but they need not be prominently introduced to the notice of every passerby.

But the message of the Great Plains landscape is clear. Only one of fifty-two sample privies was situated in front of the house, that is, between the nearest public road and the dwelling. Among several hundred regional observations, only two other cases involved a front yard privy. Interestingly, in each case the dwelling houses were small and of the kind regionally associated with temporary or migrant labor. This is not to suggest a cultural or ethnic difference, but that the property owner may have perceived different standards for the small yards and houses provided for hired laborers than for his own dwelling.

Clearly, a privy in the backyard, a "backhouse," was convenient. Chores were done here, draft animals and equipment readied for fieldwork. Logically, then, there were reasons for a privy in the backyard. But why the shunning of the front yard? Families were large and distances across farmyards great, and it was not uncommon to have more than one privy—but seldom ever in front of the house.

The public function of the front yard was evident in the privy era. Houses faced the nearest road and it was the space in front of the house that the public saw first and most closely. Accordingly, considerable effort was made to keep it presentable. The shaded front porch and adjacent yard also were functioning social space, that provided a place for neighborly conversations, occasional teas and ice cream socials, and dating. This was simply not a proper place for the privy.

It is hard to imagine our grandparents rising from the porch settee to enter a front yard privy while still in full view of guests. Equally daunting was the prospect of graciously leaving such a privy under the gaze of guests, neighbors or the passing public. Decorum dictated that one left the social arena discreetly, walked around or through the house, and sought the little house out back. An informant recalled a strategic hole in the door of their privy that allowed her to scan the yard to avoid the embarrassment of stepping out in front of a neighbor or passerby. The oft depicted, but seldom seen, moon or star in the door provided a similar benefit to the shy privy user.

Relegated to the backyard, the privy also was subject to other locational constraints. For example, a proper remoteness was valued by most homeowners, though not by public health authorities. Official thinkers lobbied for a location near the house in order to reduce "exposure" during bad weather. Actually, the concern was that people would resort to relieving themselves on the ground, especially at night or in stormy weather, instead of trekking to a remote privy. Promiscuous defecation was the real issue for it threatened the

Four Mile Community Church WPA Sanitary Privy in Teller County is an example of how easy it is to add a privacy screen. (Kenneth Jessen)

modest gains made in rural sanitation. However, decorum dictated that the issue be broached indirectly. The result was a curious but dire warning about the consequences of remote privies. One observer wrote, "Much discomfort and some digestive ills arise from the necessity—especially for women—of going a considerable distance in cold weather and at night, to such places."

The official recommendation then, was to place the privy near the house, "... 5 to 20 feet from the most convenient rear door." Ideally, the two structures would be connected by a covered walkway to further promote use during inclement weather, and a rose trellis to protect sensibilities by screening the connection between house and privy. Few rural folk, at least on the Great Plains, were sold on such bureaucratic vision.

In privy parlance, to "make a trip" was a socially acceptable euphemism for visiting the toilet. The phrase was, however, more than mere verbal disguise. At times, the distance separating dwelling and privy did indeed assume the proportions of a minor journey. In a sample of twenty-five observations, the average distance separating house and privy was 37 yards, the range of distances being 12 to 88 yards. In fact, in seven of fifty-two cases, the privy was the most remote structure in the complex of outbuildings, but in only two cases was it the nearest.

Ostensibly, it was odor that exiled the privy to far corners of the yard, yet it is curious that one often passed the pigpen or corral en route to the little house. Were massive odors of the cattle lots somehow more tolerable than those from the privy? Were privy flies—an official dread—more likely to visit the house than pigpen flies? Official recommendations notwithstanding, homeowners felt a strong need to keep the little house at a socially proper distance as a psychological buffer to protect the sensibilities of residents and visitors.

An even more unusual example of a WPA Sanitary Privy is this two-door model in Galeton. It may have been designed for use behind schools where the boys' and girls' facilities are usually separate. (Charles Collins)

Distancing privy from dwelling had to pay significant psychological rewards since it sacrificed another reward, efficiency. If one assumes an average of six daily visits for a healthy adult, compared to perhaps two visits to gather eggs or carry coal, then accumulated travel time would suggest that the privy be placed nearer the house than most other outbuildings. A basic calculation reveals that a family member might walk well over half mile each day to and from the privy! Placing the privy amidst or beyond the other outbuildings might be efficient for those outside doing chores: however, for people in the house, especially the wife and small children, and for everyone at night, the remote privy made no practical sense. Yet, allegedly it was for women and children that the privy was most important.

There is no question that many Great Plains folks tried to shield their privies from public view. Nearly 80 percent of the transect examples were situated in such a fashion that they could not be seen as one entered the farmyard. In forty-one of fifty-two cases, a visitor standing at the foot of the lane or driveway (typically beside the mailbox) could not see the outhouse because it was behind the house or some other building in the yard. The pattern is too consistent to be coincidental or random. Residents seemed determined that it not be the privy that greeted visitors nor gave

An original idea for use in the fields was to make the privy portable. The tongue can be pulled down to allow the structure to be moved and at the same time, empty its contents. What it lacks in sanitation, it makes up for in practicality. (Charles Collins)

them their initial impression of the farmstead. It was likewise important that family members be able to enter or leave the privy without the scrutiny of passing strangers or neighbors.

Another observation underscores the seeming illogic of privy placement. The second sample revealed that almost one-half of the privies were so situated that they could not be seen from the backdoor of the dwelling; familial privacy was apparently only slightly less important than public modesty. Consequently, the route that led from back step to outhouse was usually long, seldom straight and often curved out of sight before reaching its destination. For a visitor in quest of a farm privy, standing on the back step and looking was no guarantee of success. A well-worn path was the best clue. Typically, the search ended behind the barn or some shed, or in small spaces between the other structures. In a culture that has championed efficiency and convenience, and has spoken with pride of its "openness," the seclusion of the privy is a most interesting contradiction.

Some yards were too small or contained too few buildings to easily screen the privy. Still an effort was usually made to obscure the structure or at least to block direct view of the door. Rose arbors were advocated by the government, while private choice ran to quick growing clumps of tall sunflowers, hollyhocks or climbing honeysuckle—the latter sometimes referred to as privy orchids for their ability to disguise the little houses while perfuming the surrounding air. One period humorist advocated stacking the family's firewood in front of the privy. In this way, he suggested, the wood box was kept filled, especially by womenfolk who were either returning from the little house or who seeing men in the vicinity disguised their abortive trip by fetching wood. Woodpiles were indeed used to screen the privy and no doubt a good bit of wood was carried for this reason, for an armload of kindling was a handy foil to the insensitive query "where you been?"

THE FINAL ANALYSIS

Privies are disappearing faster than any other artifact structure. And we should lament the passing of the old outhouse, but not because it symbolizes a happier, simpler time. For with the disappearance of each little house another clue from the common landscape, an insight into our cultural value system is lost. As repositories of our cultural reluctance, and

The well-proportioned, gable roof outhouse on the Schaffer place near Idalia in Yuma County is pleasing to the eye and can be moved easily over a newly dug pit when necessary. (Mary Jane Groves)

often our social embarrassment, privies carry greater evidential weight than most other landscape artifacts. It is axiomatic that we reveal more about ourselves by what we try to deny than what we choose to display.

There is a tendency to look at the privy era as a time very different, a time when society was less open and more compelled by Victorian mores. But having engineered the privy from the back of the yard and into our dwellings, does it follow that we have become less inhibited and more sophisticated? Clearly, refinements in technology and convenience have occurred. But have cultural values been likewise refined? Which of our cultural devices of avoidance and disguise have we changed or discarded?

In a variety of other ways the privy and modern bathroom are closely related, as is behavior associated with them. For example, the comparatively small size of each is a statement of modesty, or at least an acknowledgement that this is not the proper way and place to "show off." Both facilities are designed for a single occupant, especially in terms of elimination. In fact, have we become more guarded? Family or multi-seat privies were rare, but did exist; but even the most avant-garde home design stops short of the cluster-stool bathroom. Other comparisons could be pursued (white as a dominant color, protection of privacy, e.g., locking doors and absence of windows, euphemistic names, privy/bathroom humor) to document that the relict privy and the contemporary bathroom are socially and culturally akin.

Originally published as "Great Plains Privies: A Micro-Geography" in *North American Culture,* 1990. Condensed version by permission of the author and publisher.

This privy at Cahone is an extreme case of remote location. It is well beyond the farthest building on this ranch and a good 100 yards from the ranch house. (Kenneth Jessen)

Appendix B: Review of Selected Outhouse Books

The Specialist

The first successful book about outhouses was *The Specialist*, written by Charles "Chic" Sales. With excellent illustrations, this book measured only 4 inches by 6 inches and contained thirty-one pages. Published in 1929, Sales used a fictional character by the name of Lem Putt. The book was based on a real person Sales knew from his hometown in Urbana, Illinois. In less than three thousand words, Sales brought Lem Putt and his homespun philosophy to light. Narrated in the first person, Putt gave the reader advice on outhouse construction.

A stage actor and comedian, Sales presented a series of talks about his fictional character. The talks were very successful. For fear of having this gem of storytelling stolen, he and two other men formed The Specialist Publishing Company in St. Louis to convert the talk into a book. In this way, the material could be copyrighted.

Sales, however, realized that a talk was different than a book. He worked hard to make every word count.

At $1 per copy, the small book was an immediate success. Sales skyrocketed and passed over one million copies. Fan mail poured into Sales with some asking for advice from the specialist. Sales answered each letter personally and responded in the vernacular of Lem Putt.

By 1934, the sales of *The Specialist* had declined to two thousand a year, and his partners gave him the exclusive rights to the book. Much to the consternation of Sales, his fans began to refer to their privies as a "Chic Sales." For a number of years, his name had replaced both "outhouse" and "privy" in American culture.

Lem Putt presented himself as a carpenter. Putt boasted of building houses, barns, churches and other structures. He found a niche, however, in the specialized construction of outhouses. Through the voice of Putt, Sales applied a lot of common sense and humor to privy construction and placement. For example, on the issue of the door:

Now, I sez, how do you want that door to swing? Openin' in or out? He said he didn't know. So I sez it should open in. This is the way it works out. Place yourself in there. The door openin' in, say about forty-five degree. This gives you air and lets the sun beat in. Now, if you hear anybody comin', you can give it a quick shove with your foot and there you are. But if she swings out, where are you? You can't run the risk of havin' her open for air or sun, because if anyone comes, you can't get up off that seat, reach way around and grab 'er without gettin' caught, now can you? He could see I was right.[1]

Sales passed away in 1936, but his remarkable book remains in print.

1. Sales, Charles. *The Specialist*. (St. Louis: Specialist Publishing Company, 1929), p. 24.

The Vanishing American Outhouse by Ronald S. Barlow
9 x 11-7/8, 136 pages, soft cover, color interior, Viking Studio, 2000
   Although there are a few minor errors, this is the premier outhouse book because it combines detailed information and excellent photography. Good examples have been selected to illustrate the text. There are also a number of historical drawings, including the WPA Sanitary Privy.

Ode to the Outhouse, Foreword by Roger Welsch
5-3/4 x 5-3/4, 108 pages, hard cover, color interior, Voyageur Press, 2002
   This excellent little book has selected works by several authors, including CBS Sunday Morning's commentator Roger Welsch. The color photographs are interesting with good captions. Postcards and drawings also are included as well as cover shots of other historic outhouse books.

Outhouses of Alaska by Harry M. Walker
8 x 6-1/2, 64 pages, hard cover, color interior, Graphic Arts Center Publications, 1996
   Individual stories and photographs on specific outhouses are covered in this excellent book. It must have taken quite a bit of time to gather all of the information.

Privies Galore by Mollie Harris
5-5/8 x 8-1/8, 135 pages, hard cover, Alan Sutton, publisher (no date)
   This British book has very good historical information with excellent photographs and good captions. The book points out the evolution of the outhouse with a lot of detail.

The Two-Story Outhouse by Norm Weis
6 x 9, 273 pages, soft cover, Caxton, 1988
   This book includes lots of history on specific outhouses all over the Rocky Mountain West, including Canada. It is well-written and well-organized by location. This book presents a level of detail not found elsewhere.

Nature Calls by Dottie Booth
7-7/8 x 8, 86 pages, soft cover, color interior, Ten Speed Press, 1998
   There are no captions to the photographs, and only some of the stories relate to the specific structures shown. However, quotations from a number of individuals make for interesting reading. Despite some weaknesses, there is a lot of good historical information and a fascinating section about outhouses around the world.

Bibliography

BOOKS

Action on the Plains. Yuma, Colorado: Yuma County Historical Society, 1958.

Bailey, Delores. *God's County U.S.A. Wall Street, Colorado.* Fort Collins, Colorado: Robinson Press Inc., 1982.

Balsley, Robert. *Early Gold Hill.* Self-published, 1971.

Bauer, William H., James L. Ozment and John H. Willard. *Colorado Post Offices*, Golden, Colorado: Colorado Railroad Museum, 1990.

Bishop, James R. *Castle Building From My Point of View*, Self-published, 2000.

Bjorklund, Linda. *Hartsel - History of a Town.* Self-published, 2001.

Bradley, Christine. *William A. Hamill.* Fort Collins, Colorado: Colorado State University Cooperative Extension Service, Historical Bulletin Number 2, 1977.

Brown, Evelyn Joan. *Early History of Montrose County, Colorado.* Gunnison, Colorado: Western State College, 1987 (Master of Arts Thesis)

Brown, Robert L. *Cripple Creek, Then and Now.* Denver: Sundance, 1991.

_____. *Jeep Trails to Colorado Ghost Towns.* Caldwell, Idaho: Caxton Printers, 1963.

_____. *Colorado Ghost Towns, Past and Present.* Caldwell, Idaho: Caxton Printers, 1977.

_____. *Ghost Towns of the Colorado Rockies*, Caldwell, Idaho: Caxton Printers, 1977,

Case, Stanley R. *The Poudre - A Photo History.* Self-published, 1995.

Crofutt, George A. *Crofutt's Grip-Sack Guide of Colorado*, (1885 Edition). Boulder, Colorado: Johnson Books, 1981 reprint.

Dallas, Sandra. *Colorado Ghost Towns and Mining Camps.* Norman, Oklahoma: University of Oklahoma Press, 1985.

Dyer, Mary. *Echoes of Como, Colorado 1879 to 1988.* George Meyer, 1975.

Eberhart, Perry. *Ghosts of the Colorado Plains.* Athens, Ohio: Swallow Press, 1986.

Feitz, Leland. *Ghost Towns of the Cripple Creek District.* Colorado Springs, Colorado: Little London Press, 1974.

Fiester, Mark. *Blasted, Beloved, Breckenridge.* Boulder, Colorado: Pruett Publishing Company, 1973.

Gillette, Jack H. *The Cheyenne Line*, Self-Published, 1997.

Gilliland, Mary Ellen. *Frisco!* Silverthorne, Colorado: Alpenrose Press, 1984.

_____. *Summit.* Silverthorne, Colorado: Alpenrose Press, 1980.

Gresham, Hazel. *North Park.* Steamboat Springs, Colorado: The Steamboat Pilot, 1975.

Griswold, Don and Jean Griswold. *Colorado's Century of "Cities".* Self-published, 1958.

_____. *History of Leadville and Lake County.* 2 vols. Denver: Colorado Historical Society, 1996.

_____. *The Carbonate Camp Called Leadville.* Denver: The University of Denver Press, 1971.

Guide to the Georgetown - Silver Plume Historic District. Evergreen, Colorado: Cordillera Press Inc., 1990.

Helmers, Dow. *Historic Alpine Tunnel.* Chicago: Swallow Press, 1963.

History of Clear Creek County. Historical Society of Idaho Springs, Denver: Specialty Publishing Inc., 1986.

History of East Morgan County. Dallas Texas: Curtis Media Corporation, 1987.

Howard, June Peterson. *Stories of Sunshine.* Longmont, Colorado: The Book Lode, 1994.

Jessen, Kenneth and Roy Paul O'Dell. *An Ear in His Pocket - The Life of Jack Slade*. Loveland, Colorado: J.V. Publications, 1996.

Jessen, Kenneth. *Ghost Towns, Colorado Style*. 3 vols. Loveland, Colorado: J.V. Publications L.L.C., 2001.

Jones, James R. "Jim." *Denver & New Orleans*, Denver: Sundance Publications Ltd, 1997.

Kelly, Suzy and Charlotte Merrifield. *Memories of St. Elmo*, Self-published, 1993.

Kempner, Helen Ashley Anderson. *Bonanza!* Colorado Springs, Colorado: Little London Press, 1978.

Kiowa County, Colorado - Centennial History. Dallas, Texas: Curtis Media Corporation, 1989.

Logan County: Better by 100 Years. Dallas, Texas: Curtis Media Corporation, 1987.

Mather, Sandra F. *Dillon - Denver and the Dam*. Breckenridge, Colorado: Summit Historical Society, 1994.

Mathews, Charles. *Early Days Around the Divide*. St. Louis, Missouri: New Era Studio, 1969.

Mesa County, Colorado - A 100 Year History. Museum of West Colorado. 1986.

Miller, Don C. *Ghosts on a Sea of Grass*. Missoula, Montana, Pictorial Histories Publishing Co., 1990.

Montgomery, Mabel Guise. *A Story of Gold Hill, Colorado*. Boulder, Colorado: The Book Lode, 1987 (reprint of the original 1930 booklet)

Mumey, Nolie. *History of Tin Cup, Colorado*. Boulder, Colorado: Johnson Publishing Company, 1963.

Munn, Bill. *A Guide to the Mines of the Cripple Creek District*. Colorado Springs, Colorado: Century One Press, 1984.

Noel, Thomas J., Paul F. Mahoney and Richard E. Stevens. *Historical Atlas of Colorado*. Norman, Oklahoma, University of Oklahoma Press, 1993.

Nossaman, Allen. *Many More Mountains*. 3 vols. Denver: Sundance Publications Ltd., 1998.

Pearce, Sarah J. and Christine Pfaff. *Guide to Historic Central City & Black Hawk*. Evergreen, Colorado: Cordillera Press Inc., 1987.

Pederson, Henry F. Jr. *'Rough it with Ease' The Story of the McGraw Ranch*, Self-published, 1990.

Perry, Eleanor. *I Remember Tin Cup*. Self-published, 1986.

Poor, M.C. *Denver, South Park & Pacific*. Denver: Rocky Mountain Railroad Club, 1976.

Propst, Nell Brown. *Forgotten People - A History of the South Platte Trail*. Boulder, Colorado: Pruett Publishing Company, 1979.

_____. *Uncommon Men and the Colorado Prairie*. Caldwell, Idaho: Caxton Printers Ltd., 1992.

Rowe, Jim and Louise. *Portal into the Past - Clear Creek Canyon of Chaffee County*. Self-published, no date given.

Schader, Conrad F. *Colorado's Alluring Tin Cup*. Golden, Colorado: Regio Alta Publications, 1992.

Shaffer, Ray. *A Guide to Places on the Colorado Prairie 1540-1975*. Boulder, Colorado: Pruett Publishing Company, 1978.

Sharp, Verna. *A History of Montezuma, Sts. John and Argentine*. Breckenridge, Colorado: Summit Historical Society, 1971.

Simmons, Virginia McConnell. *The San Luis Valley - Land of the Six-Armed Cross*. Boulder, Colorado: Pruett Publishing Company, 1979.

_____. *The Upper Arkansas*. Boulder, Colorado: Pruett Publishing Company, 1990.

_____. *Bayou Salado*. Colorado Springs, Colorado: Century One Press, 1966.

Sneed, F. Dean. *Las Animas County Ghost Towns*, Self-published, 2000.

Stampfli, Benjamin T. *Ghost Towns of the Colorado Prairies*. Fort Collins, Colorado: High Plains Reclamation-Preservation Project, 1999.

Taylor, Robert G. *Cripple Creek Mining District*. Palmer Lake, Colorado: Filter Press, 1973.

The South Park Line. Colorado Rail Annual No. 12, Golden, Colorado: The Colorado Railroad Museum, 1974.

Vandenbusche, Duane. *The Gunnison Country.* Gunnison, Colorado: B & B Printers, 1980.

Virden, William L. *Cornerstones and Communities.* Loveland, Colorado: Rodgers & Nelsen, 2001.

Watrous, Ansel. *History of Larimer County, Colorado.* Fort Collins, Colorado: The Courier Printing & Publishing Co., 1911.

Wilkins, Tiv. *Colorado Railroads.* Boulder, Colorado: Pruett Publishing Company, 1974.

Woener, Gail Hughbanks. *Willard, Colorado, A Special Place in Time.* Austin, Texas: Paisano Press, 1987.

Wolle, Muriel Sibell. *Stampede to Timberline.* Chicago: Sage Books, 1949.

_____. *Timberline Tailings.* Chicago: Sage Books, 1977.

PERIODICALS

Alice G. Milne House. Summit Historical Society, Breckenridge, Colorado at: wysiwyg://Welcome.92/http://www.summithistorical.org/MilneHouse.html.

Brungard, Sue and Carolyn Malaby. "Inter-Laken: The Past with a Future." *Water and Power,* (Water Review Quarterly) Vol. 66, No. 1 (Winter 1981).

Collins, Charles O. "Great Plains Privies: A Micro-Geography." *North American Culture,* Vol. 5. (1989). pp. 3-29.

Collins, Charles O. "The W.P.A. Privy." *Fence Post,* June 25, 2001, pp. 9-10, 103-104.

Cornelius, Coleman. "School Finger Prints Nab Suspect; Accused Peeping Tom withdraws from Regis Teaching Program." *Denver Post,* January 12, 2000. p. B4.

Ditmer, Joanne. "'Free the Bells' of Bathroom Bunker." *Denver Post,* July 15, 2001, p. D04.

Emery, Erin. "A Castle Rises in the U.S. Forest in Tribute to Working Men; Jim Bishop has Spent 3 Decades on his Stone Monument." *Denver Post,* September 3, 2001, p. A23.

Frank, Sharon. "Hey Honey! Come look at this - a whole article devoted to the study of outhouses." *Fence Post,* April 25, 1994, pp. 4-7.

Frazier, Deborah. "U.S. Forest Service's Face Not Flushed Over John's Cost." *Rocky Mountain News,* August 15, 2001, p. 7A.

Garner, Joe. "Yabba dabba...loo?" *Rocky Mountain News,* August 10, 2001.

Noel, Tom. "Colorado's World-class Outhouse." *Denver Post,* July 11, 1991, p. 7B.

"Posh Privy Flushed Priorities." *Denver Post,* August 27, 2001, p. D06.

Quillen, Ed. "Old-time Outhouse is Going Way of all Flush." *Denver Post,* October 19, 1997, p. MAG 8:4.

Ross, Lillian. "A Golden Opportunity." *Rocky Mountain News,* September 14, 2001, p. 25D (Inter-Laken).

Wall Street (Keith Maull)

Index

Alma 86
Alma Junction 87
Alpine Tunnel 149
Alta 170
Alvin 35
American Eagles Mine 107
American Smelting and Refining 130
Anaconda 108
Argentine Central 71
Atwood, Sidney 54
Austin, David 127

Barnes, David 17
Barrett, Mike 174
Barry, Vinton and Bill 108
Bearce, Gen. Horatio B. 115
Beckwith, Elton and Edwin 145
Bedrock 171
Beecher Island 36
Bell, Dr. William A. 148
Bio-Sun compositing system 186, 187
Bishop, Jim 146
Black Hawk 72
Bluma, Tony 42, 46, 48
Bonanza 159
Boston 98
Breckenridge 99
Brunot Agreement 177
Burlington & Chicago 40

Burlington & Missiouri 46, 48, 56

Cahone 198
Camp Cree 113
Capitol City 172
Cedar Hill Coal & Coke 137
Cenicero 163
Central City 74
Chaparrel RV Park 191
Chicago, Burlington & Quincy 41, 46, 56
Chivington 37
Chruch of the Latter Day Saints 165
Clarkville 38
Clark, Ted 38
Clivius-Multrum composting system 182
Cobabe, Thomas 23
Cokedale 130
Collins, Charles O. 189, 193, 196, 197
Colorado Fuel & Iron 132, 135, 136, 137, 139
Colorado Histoircal Society 87, 145, 160
Colorado Midland 93
Colorado National Guard 134
Colorado Trail 121
Colorado & Northwestern 62, 65
Columbian Exposition 155
Columbine 19
Como 88
Conejos Grant 166
Coors, Adolph 70

Cortez 173
Cowdrey, Charles 20
Crescent moon 12
Crested Butte 150
Crystal 153
Crystal Lakes 114
Cub Lake Trail 28

Dailey 39
Dempsey, Pat 54
Denver Public Library 75, 76, 100, 117, 125, 127, 137, 151, 154, 172, 180
Denver & New Orleans 50
Denver & Rio Grande 82, 160
Denver, South Park & Pacific 86, 88, 100, 141, 149, 156
Derry, Samuel 115
Dexter, James V. 120
Dillon 100
Ditmer, Joanne 187
Dove Creek 174
Dukart 18
Dumont 66
Dunn, John 50
Dunton 175

Eckles, Adams 40
Eckley 40
Eldora 58
Empire 67

Engleville 132
Evans, Augusta J. 126
Ewing 18
Ewing, Anne 142

Fairplay 89
Farncomb, Harry 102
Finntown 117
Fleming, Henry Bascom 41
Flores, Phillip E. 182, 184
Fort Garland 160
Four Mile Community Church 195
Friends of the Jackson County Library 24, 142
Frisco Historic Park 101
Fulford, Arthur 80
Fuller, J.C. 94
Futurity 118

Galeton 196
Garcia 161
Garneau, Gail and Gary 21
Gateway 176
Georgetown 68
Georgetown, Breckridge & Leadville 71
Gilfillan, John A. 58
Gilliand, Mary Ellen 105
Gilman, Henry M. 81
Glen Haven 14
Gold Hill 60
Goldfield 109
Granite 119
Great Stupa 15

Crested Butte two-story outhouse.
(Kenneth Jessen)

Gregory, John H. 72, 75, 76
Grizzly Creek comfort station 182, 184
Groseclose 189
Grover 42
Groves, Mary Jane 32, 33, 34, 36, 44, 189, 197
Guffey 90

Hahns Peak 21
Hahn, Joseph 22
Hamill House 68, 184
Hamill, William 68
Happyville 43
Harmon, Chuck 66
Harris, Mollie 11
Hartsel, Samuel 93
Hastings 133
Heartstrong 43
Helmick, Ida Lee 44
Hew Haven 47
Horsetooth Mountain Park 23
Hotchkiss, Enos 177

Idalia 44
Iliff, John 51
Inter-Laken 120
Iris 154

Janes, Alma 86
Jaroso 162
Jessen, Benjamin 119, 141, 150
Jessen, Sonje 17
Joes 45

Keller, Vick   84
Keota   46
Kircher, Lynn and Jane   162
Kitzmiller Ranch   32

La Plaza de los Manzanares   161
Labatos   163
Lace House   73
Lake City   177
Lawson, Alex   70
Leadville Boom Days   122
Lee, Abe   125
Lee, George S.   172
Lincoln City   102
Lohr/McIntosh farm   25
London Junction (see Alma Junction)
Lopez, Mike   67
Los Rinecones   164
Lucas Cemetery   33
Ludlow   134

Mahorey store   56
Malta   123
Marble   155
Maroon Creek comfort station   186
Mary Murphy Mine   124, 126
Mason, Cleve   43
Maull, Keith   28, 63, 68, 88, 127
May, William Horace   136
McGraw, John and Irene   26
Mesita   165
Methodist Church   39, 56

Miller, Cheryl   96
Miller, Lyle
Milne, Alice   99
Monster   91
Montezuma   103
Mosquito Pass   122
Mountain City   75
Moyle Brothers Band   180

National Register of Historic Places   63, 73, 96, 115, 121, 130, 135
Nederland   61
Nevadaville   76
New Jersey Zinc   81
New York Engineering Company   116
Nielson, Harry   38
Noel, Thomas   184
Nolan, William   80

Old Maid Mine   9
Oro City   125
Osgood, John C.   135, 155

Packer, Alfred   178
Pearl   27
Penitentes   164
Pennsylvania Mill   104
Peru Creek   104
Pierson, Bill   59
Pitkin, Gov. Frederick W.   156
Pueblo & State Line Railroad   49

Quillen, Ed   141

Rawley Mine and Mill   159
Raymer   48
Recen, Henry   101
Red Cliff   10, 82
Red Mountain Pass   179
Redstone   135
Ride, Sally   47
Rim Rock   36
Rockafellow, Benjamin   136
Rockdale   83
Rockvale   136
Roeschlaub, Robert   68
Rollinsville   77
Rollins, John Q. A.   77, 94
Russell Gulch   78
Russell, William Green   78
Rust, Merle W.   14

Salina   62
Salt Works   94
San Francisco   166
San Luis Southern   165, 168
Sandy Hook   159
Sangre de Cristo Grant   165
Schaffer   197
Schoeninger, Ardie   9, 99, 104, 118, 128, 134, 140, 149, 167, 175, 191
Shaw, Rex and Kris   24
Sheep Mountain Mill   153
Sheridan Lake   49

Sheridan, Gen. Phil 49
Sidney 50
Silver Cliff 148
Silver Plume 71
Silverton 180
Slade, Jack 29
Slate Creek Hall 105
Smith, Lucien K. 73
Sneed, F. Dean 132, 137, 139, 140
Snyder, J. W. 51
Soux, Bill and Colleen 90
Squaw Mountain 192
Stanley, Clyde 46
Stratton, William S. 107
St. Elmo 126
Summit Historical Society 99
Summitville 167
Sunshine 63

Tabor, H. A. W. 123, 125
Tarryall 96
The Old Privy advertisement 16
Theresa Mine 111
Thomas, Lowell 112
Thompson, Ron 135
Tincup 158
Tollerburg 137
Toller, Giacomo 137
Tressie C Mine 124
Trombly, Cyndi 124, 179
Turret 127
Twin Lakes 128

Union Pacific 51, 185
U.S. Forest Service 121, 159, 186

Valdez, Gabriel 139
Vallorso 140
Vernon, James J. 53
Vicksburg 84
Victor 112
Victor and Cripple Creek Gold Mining Company 107
Victor-American Fuel Company 133
Viejo San Acacio 168
Virginia Dale Stage Staion 29
Virginia Dale Commnunity Church 30

Wall Street 64
Wapiti 106
Ward, Calvin M. 65
Wauneta 34, 54
Weis, Norman 150
Weldona 55
Westcliffe 148
West, Vern 9
Wheeler, Pearl 27
Willard, Daniel A. 56
Winfield 85
Wolle, Muriel Sibell 117, 151, 154, 172
Woods, Frank and Harry 112
Woodward, Mike and Beth 151
WPA Sanity Privy 33, 34, 38, 50, 52, 54, 67, 74, 90, 97, 132, 134, 189, 194
Wray, City of 34

Bonanza (Kenneth Jessen)

OTHER BOOKS BY KENNETH JESSEN

Ghost Towns, Colorado Style, Volume One - Northern Region
Ghost Towns, Colorado Style, Volume Two - Central Region
Ghost Towns, Colorado Style, Volume Three - Southern Region
Bizarre Colorado
Eccentric Colorado
Colorado Gunsmoke
Estes Park - A Quick History
Georgetown - A Quick History
An Ear in His Pocket
Railroads of Northern Colorado
Thompson Valley Tales
How It All Began: Hewlett-Packard's Loveland Facility

 2212 Flora Court Loveland, CO 80537